Third Edition
1984

# The
# Newsletter Editor's Desk Book

*Marvin Arth &*
*Helen Ashmore*

ISBN: 0-938270-03-6
Library of Congress Catalog No. 81-83398
Printed in the United States of America

Published by Parkway Press
Box 8158
Shawnee Mission, Kansas 66208

# DEDICATION

Professional journalists are putting out thousands of good newsletters in this country. They know what they're doing, and this book will serve more to *remind* than *inform* them. There is, however, little specific academic training for newsletter editing, so even an experienced editor may find this modest reference handy. Some top public relations professionals have reported that they use this book for reference in their work. That's gratifying, and we hope that *The Newsletter Editor's Desk Book* will become the "little book" of newsletter editing—that is, both the tidiest and the most highly respected reference on its subject, an asset to editors of every skill level.

There are also thousands of inexperienced editors of modest news publications that yield little compensation in worldy goods or glory. The volunteer publicity person for a special interest group or club; the association executive who is essentially a one-person staff; an assistant or secretary who is *volunteered* to do the company news—anyone around who looks able to do the job may suddenly one day become a news editor.

These people are on the line. With little—sometimes no—journalistic training, they are expected to put out good newsletters, often in their "spare time" from a host of other pressing duties. It is for such editors that this book is primarly intended. We hope that it will enable them to resolve the many issues they face —or at least to know in concrete terms what the issues are—and to put out quality newsletters with a minimum of anxiety and a maximum of pleasure in a job well done.

*Marvin Arth*
*Helen Ashmore*

# Contents

**How To Use This Book**        ix

**Foreword**        1
  The Private Newspaper  1

**1/Who Needs a Newsletter?** . . . . . . . . . . . . . . . . . . . . . . . . 5
  Do We Need a Newsletter?  5
  What Do We Expect From It?  6
  Who's Going To Read It?  7
  The Newsletter in the Public Relations Context  8
  The Newsletter That *Is* the Program  9

**2/Get Organized and Get Help** . . . . . . . . . . . . . . . . . . . . . 13
  Who's Going To Do What?  13
  Are There Reporters, Photographers, Equipment
     in the House?  13
  Training Reporters  15
  Help from Outside Professionals  16
  Typewritten vs. Typeset News  17
  Who's In Charge?  21
  The Boss Who Can't Let Go  22

**3/Target the News** . . . . . . . . . . . . . . . . . . . . . . . . . . . . . . 27
  Is There News in a Newsletter?  27
  Inside News Sources  27
  Outside News Sources  29
  Series and Features  30
  The Employee Publication  33
  The Editor as Advocate  37

**4/Write, Rewrite, and Edit** . . . . . . . . . . . . . . . . . . . . . . . . 41
  Journalistic Objectivity  41
  Gathering News  41
  The Interview  42
  Approaches to Writing News Stories  47
  The Essential Stylebook  50
  Elements of News Writing  53
  Writing Good Leads  57
  Writing the Body  60
  Rewriting a Story  62
  Credibility  62
  Legal Considerations  63
  Elements of Editing  65

**5/Headlines** . . . . . . . . . . . . . . . . . . . . . . . . . . . . . . . . . . .71
The Importance of Headlines  71
Writing Good Headlines  71
Establishing Headline Styles  77
Making Headlines Fit  79

**6/Format and Makeup** . . . . . . . . . . . . . . . . . . . . . . . . . . .85
Readability and the Right "Look"  85
Paper  85
Typography  86
Elements of Makeup  94
Putting It All Together  100

**7/Production and Distribution** . . . . . . . . . . . . . . . . . . .109
Pasteup  109
Copying and Printing  112
Distribution  113

**Appendix 1/Model Stylebook** . . . . . . . . . . . . . . . . . . . .119
General Manuscript Preparation  119
Punctuation  119
Capitalization  124
Spelling  126
Abbreviations  130
Numbers  131
Grammar  133

**Appendix 2/Model Headline Schedule** . . . . . . . . . . . . .143

**Appendix 3/Formula Stories** . . . . . . . . . . . . . . . . . . . . .151
Personnel Items  151
Meetings  152
Speeches  153
Reports  154
Notices  155
Controversies  156

**Appendix 4/Form Contract** . . . . . . . . . . . . . . . . . . . . . .161

**Appendix 5/Copy Editing Marks
and Typesetting Specifications** . . . . . . . . . . . . . . . . .169

# HOW TO USE THIS BOOK

If you edit a special-audience newsletter or newspaper, this book will help you. It does not matter if you are the most or least experienced journalist on earth, if you type the news yourself and hand it out to 30 Friends of the Teapot, or do Amalgamated International's Corporate News—typeset and mailed to 250,000 people. A newsletter is a special form of communication and this is a special book jam-packed with information about that form.

A newsletter is, by nature and history, a modest, special-audience, private newspaper. If you are a novice editor, don't be intimidated by the many suggestions between these covers. Don't feel that, in your first issue after you get the book you must suddenly do everything as well as a veteran newspaper editor does, according to the principles of classical journalism set forth here. Do what seems to you to be most important. Do things in order, for your readers.

Unless you have the skills and the need to do an elaborate multicolumn layout, skip the chapters on that subject, at least for now. If you put out a brightly written, cleanly produced *letter*, with *news* in it, you'll have readers and you'll be serving them well. A *news letter* that is typed and looks like a letter conveys a personal feeling and an immediacy that typeset newsletters do not. Don't be ashamed to send out good typed newsletters. They work.

*Trouble with typewritten newsletters comes, usually, from single-spacing long and badly written stories, then sending out many crowded pages of these visual and intellectual offenses.* The unhappy, would-be reader sinks into the mire. (If you typewrite across the page, then double-space, use some underlining, write the news brightly and briefly, and limit the number of pages to two or three. This works just fine for Mr. Kiplinger. It can work for you.)

No matter what your editing skills and ambitions, you will get the most out of this book if you will first sit down with the last few issues of your newsletter, school newspaper, membership or other special-audience publication and seriously gauge its strengths and weaknesses. Is it interesting? Is it well-written? Is it accurate? Are facts and figures, including contact phone numbers and dates, times and locations of future events *right*? How does it look? How are the headlines? *Give yourself a hearty pat on the back for its good points.* Then map out a plan to attack its failings, at a reasonable rate. Use this book, in other words, so that it helps you, with your own publication, and at your own pace.

# FOREWORD

## The Private Newspaper

A newletter is a private newspaper that conveys specific information to a specific audience. It influences the reader's perception of the publishing organization, and anticipated reader response is assent or support in any form, from hard cash to increased loyalty toward and effort for the publishing organization.

Newsletters are being published all over the world—by everyone from powerful multinational corporations to scrappy entrepreneuers working alone at home. These publications differ greatly, therefore, in format, content, audience and purpose.

They may be a single page or many pages. They vary in format from a tiny 4½x6 inches, to broadsheet, newspaper size of 22x35 inches. Most, as the name implies, are letter-sized.

Some are so big and so expensively produced—four-color printing on glossy paper, with photographs, artwork, and elaborate typography—that people call them magazines. Most employee organization or member association "magazines" are newsletters in fancy dress. School newspapers are in many respects like newsletters.

Newsletters may have 30 readers or 300,000. They may be written in conversational chit-chat style, in jargon, or in formal, classical prose. They have many purposes: to inform, share, persuade, promote, sell, reminisce, boost morale, solicit money—or any combination of these.

Most are published monthly, some weekly or daily; some have no set frequency. Probably the most famous irregular frequency publication was written by the late Theodore Bernstein, assistant managing editor of *The New York Times*. His mimeographed letter identified the best and the worst headlines, leads, and story writing in that newspaper. "Winners and Sinners" was intended for internal circulation at *The Times*, but gained an audience in newsrooms and journalism schools throughout America. At the bottom of the letter was a notice, "W&S is issued occasionally from the southeast corner of *The New York Times* newsroom."

Some newsletters look more like brochures or advertising flyers, the kind mailed with bills by public utilities, credit card companies and large department stores. Some carry advertising, some charge subscription prices; but most are financed by their sponsors—private industry, banks, insurance companies, professional and trade associations, cities, townships, government agencies, colleges, schools, churches, special interest groups, unions, social clubs and entrepreneurs.

The newsletter editor must make many decisions about the format, makeup, paper size, texture and color, and the typeface that will best serve the publication's purpose. But *it is content that makes a newsletter a newsletter*, that sets it off from the general newspaper or the promotional advertising brochure. The newsletter seems to fall somewhere between those two forms of communication. All newsletters involve gathering stories, writing and editing, copying and distributing, just as newspapers do. But, like advertising flyers, all are in one sense or another, selling something to their particular audience.

The audience for most newsletters share a common interest: they all go to the same school, have money in the same bank, have Corvairs, served in the same World War II outfit, work at the same place, or belong to the same club or church. A large company or professional association newsletter often addresses more than one public. The typical wide-audience publication is read by people with varying interests: employees or members and management, their families, stockholders, customers, the competition, and other interested people. Identifying and keeping readers for a newsletter is the editor's job. Only when the editor does this job can the newsletter do its job—get the right message across to the right audience.

# 1
# Who Needs
# a Newsletter?

# WHO NEEDS A NEWSLETTER?

## Do We Need a Newsletter?

"Do we need a newsletter?" you rightfully ask. Publishing one on a regular basis can be time-consuming and costly. Could the time and money be better spent on other forms of communication? More frequent meetings and personal contact, bulletin boards, a simple calendar of events? How about computer programs or audiovisual presentations? Closed circuit television? Could the target audience be reached more effectively by telegrams, letters, telephone calls? Perhaps a combination of these approaches will serve your needs.

In many cases, however, a newsletter is the most effective and economical way to reach those you want to reach with the information you want them to have. If your group has grown so large that personal communication among its members has become unlikely, difficult or impossible, a newsletter can help overcome the problem. *A newsletter can provide a sense of continuity and community to an organization of any size or character.*

Every business, association, school, church, and club of any size at all in this country has a newsletter, a powerful indication that people like private news. A newsletter is crucially important in the following instances:

If members are so scattered that close communication is difficult, a newsletter can provide a communicating link.

If members need certain detailed or technical information on a regular basis, a newsletter can provide it.

If certain goals must be promoted among a group, a newsletter can examine and explain those goals to all the readers.

If an organization depends on continuing contact with members or customers, a newsletter can remind them of the services provided by an organization.

A newsletter in these cases is the right medium for the message. *When the mass media ignores a message because of its "limited audience" appeal, chances are that audience is properly a newsletter audience. . .that the newsletter is the most efficient, economical way to reach them.*

## What Do We Expect From It?

Once it has been determined that the newsletter is the best way to get your news to your readers, the interested purpose the newsletter will serve should be carefully considered.

The purpose can be general or specific, and need not be rigidly fixed. But it should be clear—clear enough to leave no room for doubt about what it is intended to accomplish. If you are uncertain, the newsletter will reflect this uncertainty.

These are examples of general purpose:

1. To improve image, attract money and other forms of support.
2. To motivate readers: improve employee morale, increase productivity, attract new members, strengthen loyalties.

These are examples of specific purpose:

1. To advise members of a rural cooperative of energy savings techniques.
2. To attract customers to a bank—and keep them.

An editor who understands the purpose of the newsletter does not have to agonize over questions involving content. Why should we run this story? What general or specific purpose does it serve? If, for instance, the purpose of a newsletter is to keep members convinced of the worth and vitality of an organization, then personal items about employees are out of place.

But if the purpose is to build employee morale, encourage camaraderie and open communications among a large staff—say in a metropolitan hospital—then personal items as well as stories about the superior services of the hospital are proper.

One purpose served by the newsletter, and of which editors do not always seem to be conscious, is that of projecting the image of the organization. What image do you wish to convey to readers? Decide. (Decide with other people who have something to say about it.)

A hospital employee relations department may wish to convey a sense of family and community, so it prints a colorful, chatty, casual publication that appeals to average employees, one that talks *about* and *to*, not *down to* them.

A government agency may wish to convey an image of economy to its taxpaying readers—they are, after all, footing the bill. So they print black on inexpensive white standard-size paper and avoid frills. The tone of the writing is serious; they wish to project competence, not frivolousness.

An investment firm wishes to project affluence, so it uses flashy artwork and color combinations, unusual paper size and texture to project unique success, to suggest to customers that this firm is indeed where all the right money is. A professional association that wishes to attract new members may use high-toned graphics and handsome paper to convey "prestige."

## Who's Going to Read It?

The wise editor keeps readers clearly in mind. But for some editors this isn't as easy as it may sound.

It's easy enough for the entrepreneur who edits a newsletter on how to invest in gold coins. He probably works alone or with a very small staff. He has one audience—people who want to make money in gold. He has one purpose—to tell them how to do that. Pleasing board members, sales people or secretaries is not his goal.

At the other end of the spectrum is the editor of the large hospital or insurance company newsletter with multiple audiences to please. While all parties share a common interest in the organization's activities and well-being, each group has a specific interest. Hospital board members, for instance, want to see the bottom line figures from the annual report. The employees in housekeeping want to know who's getting married. The doctors want to see themselves receiving awards from professional associations.

An editor of such a multiple audience publication can clarify the picture by counting audiences—in a list. Who does it go to? Why? Who's more important in this line up? The sales force? The clerical staff? The board? The clients? Which stories in the last newsletter were of interest to all parties? Which ones to one group only? *Is the newsletter written largely for one group at the expense of having the others become unhappy unreaders?*

It is not always possible to satisfy widely different audiences with the same publication. Sometimes it becomes necessary to publish two newsletters—one internal, chiefly for employees or members, and one external, for the general public. Many large organizations do this. Employees or members receive both newsletters, but outsiders do not receive the insiders' newsletter. The fact is that the stockholder, although he may be a very nice person, does not care if Marylou in Reinsurance is having a baby shower for Sueanne in Bookkeeping.

The smaller the organization, the more likely one newsletter will serve it. By the time it grows considerably, it will probably have two newsletters—the external one and a monthly, weekly or even, in some large companies, a daily newssheet telling what's for lunch and where to sign up for baseball tickets.

## The Newsletter in the Public Relations Context

It is said that *to succeed an organization should do the right thing and let people know about it.* Letting people know about it is a function of public relations. A public relations department or person provides the mass media with news releases, texts of important speeches, notices of significant meetings and conventions, of the results of those meetings, and notices of policy changes. The general public may be reached through annual reports, films, and slide shows.

Public relations people should cooperate, not put up barriers, in their dealing with the mass media and the public at large, remembering, however, that their first obligation is always to the organization they serve.

But the organization has a specific audience that cannot always be reached through the mass media. It is reached through a newsletter.

## The Newsletter That Is The Program

Newsletters that go to widely scattered readers who rarely see one another are crucial to the reader's perception of the publishing organization. They set the tone for, define the organization for subscribers or members. In fact, in a sense, such newsletters quite often *are* to readers the associations or businesses they represent. Thoughtful planning of these publications is, therefore, is especially important. Be sure they project the image you want to project.

# 2
# Get Organized
# & Get Help

# GET ORGANIZED AND GET HELP

## Who's Going To Do What?

Some editors—of major industry publications, for instance—
are primarily top-level managers. They command a force of
professional writers, copy editors, photographers and graphic
artists. They have in-house typesetters and printers at their call,
and a mailing staff or service that gets the newsletter out pronto
once it's printed.

Other editors command no such force. Rather, they *are* the
force. Like Peter Sellers in *The Mouse That Roared*, they play all
the significant roles in the show. The editor is also the writer,
photographer, artist, typist, copier and mail clerk—and, perhaps,
the company owner.

This chapter is primarily for those editors who fall somewhere
between these two extremes—who work for a middle-sized,
perhaps growing, organization where some help is available from
members or the staff and/or from contracted outside services.

In these organizations, many questions come up about who
should do what to make the newsletter the best possible product
at the lowest possible cost.

## Are There Reporters, Photographers, Equipment in the House?

To identify and manage available resources, you, the editor,
first assess your own strengths and skills. Other publicity duties
may be many, so you must determine how much time you can
realistically devote to the newsletter. Then look around the

organization to see where talented help may be forthcoming.

If the organization is getting large, is it practical to track down every single news item yourself? Or is this a problem—taking more time than it should? Then are there enough enthusiastic, bright people to make a reporter system feasible? Volunteer *stringers*, i.e., reporters in far-flung offices or chapters, can do valuable legwork collecting routine information. They can suggest tips for stories; and occasionally a stringer turns up who is talented enough to write the stories, too.

If, in your assessment of your own strengths and skills, you admit you really are not a good photographer, there's probably a talented photography buff close by. What about Maria, the lawyer, who just won a city award for best amateur art photography? Would she help shoot photos for publication? Or Sam, the treasurer—he's good at layout and pasteup—a natural (which many an editor is not).

This kind of duty adds prestige and variety to routine work. People like to be published. It can't hurt morale to get some people involved.

As you assess the eager talent that may be available for sprucing up the newsletter operation, look around at the existing equipment to see what might contribute to the newsletter's overall quality.

Is there a typesetting machine? A printing press? Will they produce good quality headlines and photographs? Are there people in the group who can operate such equipment? Do they have time to work newsletter production into their regular schedules?

With a company newsletter, the questions from management's point of view are: Will newsletter assignments bolster or bore workers assigned to other duties? Do they have time for them? Ask potential contributors. Ask their supervisors. Let management make the decision. The question from the editor's point of view is: Will this person be more help than hindrance? *Decide before you ask for his or her help on the publication.*

Each organization has its unique combination of talent and equipment with varying capabilities. Perhaps there is little talent to tap, but if you need reporters badly, it may be worth your time to train some. This will be especially challenging if you have departments or chapters or affiliates from Maine to Mexico. Think of the bright side. If you can't train people long-distance, you've just added travel to your job description.

## Training Reporters

Reporters scattered throughout the organization—and sometimes throughout the country—are on the spot to turn up information and story ideas in their corner of the organization, where the editor cannot always be.

The problems to be worked out in dealing with these volunteers are real, but they are not insurmountable.

Bright, enthusiastic reporters turn stories in on time for each issue, then eagerly await the sight of their precious words in print. But they are not news writers. Their stories must be substantially rewritten before they see print. If their feelings are hurt by editing—and whose are not?—they may lose interest in scavenging news for you. If you need them and value them, you must help them.

This will take time. The editor must sit down with reporters, thank them, compliment them on the value of their story content, and explain how a story is reworked into newspaper style. The editor, who goes over a reporter's story, explaining from the lead to the end the importance of journalistic techniques, has taken the first step to develop the reporter into a valuable writer. It will take several sessions, but with the right attitude on both parts, it will pay off.

Other reporters won't submit stories regularly, or will always be late. Another problem reporter is the one who submits stories not only late, but also with most of the facts missing. . . "to be filled in later." When? It's already past deadline!

The editor can set an early deadline for articles from such a reporter, so there will be time to complete stories for publication. Reporters who understand that incomplete stories cause delays, cost money, and may in fact be unusable, will probably cooperate more willingly. Appeal to their sense of professional obligation. If this doesn't work, replace them.

It takes time and skill, but an editor can develop a good, reliable team of reporters who regularly help cover the organization's news. It's essential to continually encourage volunteer writers to be professional enough to take their writing and their deadlines seriously.

Set realistic deadlines—not so close to publication that it is always a hassle to get the copy into print in time, yet not so far in advance that no one takes them seriously.

A strong editor has the courage—and the back-up copy—to throw out, or at least delay until a later issue, any story, photograph or piece of art submitted after a deadline. This practice encourages contributors to take deadlines seriously.

Reporters, photographers, and artists within the organization may be able to provide the quality of work required for the newsletter. But sometimes they cannot.

## Help From Outside Professionals

Sometimes a newsletter outgrows an editor with a volunteer staff. There's more, or more exacting, work than they can do well. Perhaps the editor identifies one area in which the newsletter is always weak. Photographs may not be sharp and in focus. The copying machine may be making the end product of all the work that goes into the publication look shoddy and amateurish.

The editor faced with such problems has two choices: (1) to ask for additional professional staff or equipment, or (2) to contract for services with outside firms.

If the cost-effective choice is to hire staff or to buy equipment, the editor must consider how much responsibility and time this adds to an already long list of duties. It is nearly always a mistake to buy such expensive equipment as typesetting machines or printing presses unless they are to be used for many other projects besides the newsletter. In addition to the cost of the equipment itself, other expenses such as supplies, maintenance and paying an operator must be considered. A newsletter alone can seldom justify such expenditures.

Outside writing help can be bought—from individual freelancers, public relations firms or advertising agencies.

These are expensive. They are usually not practical for collecting routine information. But for feature articles, the outside professional writer who understands the organization and its goals can provide fresh, crisp copy for the newsletter.

Likewise, professional photographers and artists, properly directed by an editor, can vastly improve the graphic quality of a newsletter. They are professionals for a reason. That reason is ostensibly that they are good. They are also expensive. Shop around.

The editor seeking outside help needs to: (1) sit down with several professional photographers and writers and look at their portfolios, (2) assess their abilities in terms of the newsletter's purpose, (3) get a clear understanding of their charges, and (4) clear any contracts with the organization's bigwigs.

## Typewritten vs. Typeset News

If you consider outside printing and typesetting, the main thing you are going to look at is cost. Get some estimates and bids.

A typesetter estimates that typesetting a four-page newsletter will cost $25-$35 per page. A printer estimates that printing 2,000 newsletters will cost $200 plus $7.50 for each half-tone (for photographs). A layout and pasteup artist bids $50 for monthly services.

"Too much," you say. "We'll continue doing it the way we've been doing it." You may want to consider hidden cost factors.

1. If the typist is paid $5 to $7 an hour, and if it takes ten to twenty hours to type each newsletter, getting the margins just so, making corrections, changing whole pages when some last-minute copy change is made, then the typewritten newsletter is not cheap.

Chances are that it will cost little more to have the newsletter typeset under such circumstances, and that the difference will be money well spent.

2. Using a copier may cost from 2 to 5 cents a page, plus an additional penny a sheet for the paper. Say a four-page newsletter is two sheets printed on both sides, and the cost per photocopy is 4 cents. The cost of copying each newsletter will be 16 cents, or $320 for 2,000 newsletters.

3. The figures are even more compelling when you consider that typeset copy fills only about half the space occupied by the same amount of typewritten copy. A four-page typewritten newsletter is two pages when typeset. On larger circulation newsletters, typesetting may result in sizable savings on paper and postage costs.

Another consideration is that each printed page requires a master plate, and once that plate is prepared, the printer can run off innumerable copies. The more copies printed, the lower the cost per copy, since the fixed price of the plate is distributed over the total press run. The bigger the circulation, the more the cost advantage of typesetting/printing.

A careful analysis may show that it costs no more, or only slightly more, to have a professionally typeset/printed newsletter. The quality improvement may easily justify the slightly higher cost.

This is not to say that typesetting/printing is the only way to go. Even a modest newsletter, written, edited and typed entirely by the editor and reproduced on the office copying machine, may be excellent for its purpose and circulation. It may look good and speak well to the readers it serves.

## The Typewritten Newsletter

Typewritten newsletters tend to get apologized for. "It's not much to look at," the editor says, "we just typewrite it." And, for sure, some typewritten newsletters are nothing to brag about—the ones typed in single spaced lines completely across each page. Such a solid "gray" page is uninviting.

But some very appealing publications are typewritten. The famous Kiplinger newsletter is typewritten—or it *looks* like it is. *Happenings*, the employee newsletter of a hospital in Lima, Ohio, is attractive and readable, and it is done on an ordinary typewriter, in three columns. Headlines are done in *press type*, rub-on letters, and layout is almost elegantly spare. It is bright and inviting, has plenty of white space, strong but not overwhelming graphics, and simple, abbreviated copy. Photographs are in focus, and appealing orginal drawings give it added flair. It is printed offset, which gives it access to such design elements as screening.

The handsome typewritten publication, like the handsome typeset one, conforms to the four basic principles of design.

•The page is balanced. No part of the design dominates so as to outweigh the other parts.

•The page has contrast. If it were too white or too gray, it would seem lifeless.

•The page has unity. Although materials relate to separate stories or items, they work together visually.

•The page has proportion. As you compose a page, thinking of it in thirds, rather than in halves or quarters, generally gives pleasing results.

If you have access to an electronic typewriter or word processor, learn to use it. It will allow you to correct copy electronically—with the touch of one or more buttons—and speed up the writing process considerably on a typewritten newsletter.

One distinct advantage of the typewritten newsletter is that it looks timely and personal. If it is a daily, with content so timely that any delay in reaching readers will render the news valueless, then typewriting is probably preferable to typesetting.

## The Typeset Newsletter

Typesetting assures good-looking, professional copy, with evenly spaced words and, if you want them, justified margins. Typesetting takes time and money because it requires another professional person's time (the typesetter's) and a lot of going back and forth of copy from editor to typesetter. Each change of hands provides opportunity for error, loss, and change of mind—for spending more time and more money.

First, typewritten final copy goes to the typesetter. A keyboard operator enters it into a phototypesetting machine and, more than likely, makes a few mistakes in doing so. A proofreader reads the typeset copy and notes errors.

You get a photocopy or "proof" of the typeset, proofed (meaning proofread) copy—now in long columns called galleys. You proof them, too—and find mistakes of your own, mistakes of fact, grammar, omission. Or, perhaps, since it's been a few days since you've seen what you wrote, you decide you want to say something in a different way. (This is unacceptable professional behavior, and we all do it. It costs more time, more money.)

You send corrected galley proofs back to the typesetter who corrects them and sends "second generation" (corrected) proofs back to you. Ideally you don't change your mind about anything this time; errors have been ferreted out, and layout can begin. In fact, a couple of small errors are usually detected, and the typesetter makes final—this time we mean it—corrections before makeup can begin.

Typesetting and printing offer the advantage of opportunity for variety in page makeup, and for crisp-looking, readable copy. A good, clean, readable page is what we're all after.

## Who's In Charge?

Once the editor has a good staff organized from talented help inside and outside the organization, the newsletter ought to be looking good and doing its job. One thing that can slow down the whole process, however, is confusion about who's in charge. You may think you are. Chances are you are not. You have the responsibility all right. But you do not have free reign to call all the shots about costs and contents of the newsletter. Not at first.

Almost invariably someone else has the final say about the budget and editorial content of the newsletter. And that someone may be one or—heaven help you—more bosses, or even a board.

Your relationship with whoever has final say about the newsletter is crucial to your—and the newsletter's—continuing success.

There are several typical problems in the editor/management relationship that may be resolved with immediate action.

1. When more than one person has "final authority" and there is conflict between them, the editor should sit down with them and reach a working agreement, preferably in writing, about who does have final authority. Ideally, they will agree on *one person* for this role.

2. When policies exist about bidding for typesetting, printing, mailing, and dealing with other suppliers, the editor should discuss these with management and make sure they have a clear mutual understanding of what these policies are.

Many government agencies and organizations that do business with the government, for instance, have specific quota requirements for minority contractors. They have a set amount of money over which bids must be taken or board approval secured before expenditures can be made. Editors who do not understand and comply with such requirements can cause problems for themselves and their organizations.

The editor and executive should agree on their understanding of these policies. And they should reach mutual understanding about how far within the confines of these policies the editor's authority properly extends.

3. When the person with final authority tries to control not only budget and editorial content, but also such details as format and other newsletter specifications, it is wise to discuss any changes in these in advance of radical revisions. In general, it's a good idea to keep executives informed well in advance of all policy changes and decisions to which they must give approval.

4. When the final authority is too slow or too busy to sign off stories, get copy to him or her as early as possible. Keep checking back regularly—just short of badgering—to get approval in time for deadline.

It's not unusual—although it is unfortunate—to have a final authority who insists on changing stories after they've been typeset. The editor must convince such an executive that the time for changes is *before the copy goes to the typesetter*—that after copy is typeset any but the most essential typographic or content error corrections are far too costly in both time and money.

5. One regular contributor to many newsletters is the executive who has a monthly letter or column. Executives are a special case. But the editor must be as firm with executives as with other contributors. Teach even your biggest big bosses to meet deadlines, and help them with their writing as much as they are willing to let you. They'll appreciate your professionalism on behalf of the organization.

## The Boss Who Can't Let Go

Some executives can't seem to let go of any authority for the newsletter—as they probably can't let go of authority for anything else in the organization. This boss has management skills to develop. Meanwhile, editors can help. But first the editor must understand the boss.

The executive wants to have final say not only about his or her monthly message to readers, but about every aspect of the newsletter from budgeting and editorial content to sentence construction.

You can understand this. The executive is the person with the high public profile. The external newsletter represents the organization to the public. Employees and members perceive their organization primarily through the insiders' newsletter. These newsletters are important. The executive wants to make sure they're doing the job envisioned for them.

For this reason, the number of editors who are able to walk into a job and instantly have complete say about what goes into "their" newsletter are very few.

It isn't easy, but you can wrest this overweening concern from the boss and return it to its proper sphere—yours. You not only can do it, you must do it. It's extremely important to reach the point at which the executive has the confidence in your judgment and ability to stop interfering with your work.

Work to establish a healthy rapport with executives. Exude knowledgeable professionalism, control and confidence. Learn how they think and what they want—and act on it.

Only when executives feel an editor's intensely alert loyalty to the organization (which is to say the boss's own philosophy) will they loosen the strings on the editorial content and budget.

It's a great day in the life of the executive and editor alike when this happens, for then they are free to go about their respective duties.

Remember, such executives don't think they want you to have responsibility for their newsletter. But they do. And the editor who wrests it away will be paid for this competence many times over.

A parting thought: Don't run the boss's column on the front page with a standing head (Message from the Chair, etc.) and a mugshot. Even if your bigwig doesn't know better, you should.

# 3
# Target the News

# TARGET THE NEWS

## Is There News In A Newsletter?

In the big, worldly sense, there's probably not much news in a newsletter—not like there is, say, in *The New York Times*.

*The Times* reflects the great world—it is, in fact, a "paper of record," which means it tries to record *all the significant events in the world each day*. A big job. A great paper.

Newsletters don't have such a big job. And it would probably be a contradiction in terms to speak of "a great newsletter," because they reflect a relatively small world. But there can be very good newsletters. And very good newsletters reflect the world of their readers.

Many organizations are practically a world unto themselves. People working in a large hospital, insurance company—any large institution or business—reflect the organization's values and philosophy. They think in company terms, unconsciously, perhaps speak the company jargon. They are in many ways a true community. Association members, likewise, although often distant physically, are philosophically or socially a community.

What's news in your community? Everything is "news" to someone. The trick is to recognize what's news to your readers.

## Inside News Sources

Some reliable sources of legitimate news inside almost any organization are listed below. Editors may gather such news themselves; in a very large association or company, they may enlist contacts—stringer reporters—to help gather it.

*Meetings.* Significant meetings involving progress or policy, such as regular monthly board meetings, reveal some information that will be of interest to newsletter readers. Professional association meetings and conventions, attended by one or more staff members, provide newsworthy reports. Ideally the editor covers all important meetings in person, to catch the spirit of the occasion (if any) and such details and lively dialogue as are not captured in official minutes.

When minutes or secondhand accounts of meetings are all the editor has to work with, an interview with one or more of the participants should add some life and color to a meeting story.

*Reports.* Different departments or chapters issue reports from time to time. These reports at first glance may seem obscure, even opaque—boring beyond belief. But reports can be searched for items of actual significance to the people in the organization. An interview with the person who prepared the new budget may net explanations and quotes that will clarify the meaning of those rows of statistics in the lives of employees or members.

*Management and Personnel Announcements.* Announcements of major expansion or construction are, of course, cause for front page coverage, as are the occasions of major awards, grants or contracts involving the organization.

Memos about new policies, reports about revised programs, announcements of expanded services, additional products, or new equipment should be examined for possible stories—or short story items at the least.

Good reporters read between the lines of the seemingly insignificant announcement and interview management for details and quotes to get a story that will interest readers.

Even such a seemingly routine event as the purchase of a new copier may make a news story. The salesman or installer may be quoted explaining how it works, what it is going to do that the old copier would not do, and how it will make life easier for employees. It is not a front page story, but it's a story.

The personnel department is a prime source for stories of new employees, promotions, transfers, retirements; it's good for items about changes in work and vacation schedules, improvements in insurance and other benefits.

*Speeches.* Top officers frequently give speeches at national meetings or to local groups such as the Kiwanis Club. Often the newsletter editor helps write the speech. Do not overlook speeches as a good source of news stories, even if you did write them!

## Outside News Sources

As no man is an island, no organization is an island. The world of the newsletter may be small, but it is not closed. It is affected by laws. It is affected by attitudes and trends.

*News from the Lawmakers.* State, local and federal government bodies regulate and/or support many industries and agencies. They are constantly brewing new regulations and passing new laws that affect the nation's businesses and professional organizations. They can make or break programs overnight. The upshot of complicated regulations can be garnered from such publications as the daily *Federal Register*, and communicated to an interested audience in plain English. This is not easy. But the conscientious editor will learn to interpret, or find someone on the staff who knows how to interpret, significant rules and regulations affecting his organization.

For government agencies and federally funded programs, this information is not only of interest, it is vital.

*News from other publications.* Readers want and need to know about related industries and professional organizations throughout the country. Physical therapists are interested in developments and news about the health care industry at large. Contractors want to know about improvements in cement-mixing techniques and about interest rates on home loans. Editors scan trade publications for new developments, ideas and information.

Stories may be written from these sources, quoting the source and emphasizing how the local organization is affected by the news.

Quoting a knowledgeable source within the local organization is always a good practice to bring sharp focus to such a story.

*News of national and international import.* Reporting such news is not ordinarily the task of the organizational newsletter. But if oil prices rising in Saudi Arabia or gold prices falling in London directly affect your organization in some identifiable way, the newsletter properly reports on that effect.

Such a report is not written off the top of the editor's head. Interpretation by the president or the financial officer or the board chairman—a responsible, authoritative spokesperson—is proper. The story can be an interview, or a composite of opinions from various sources. An editor who is particularly well versed in the subject may want to add his or her own analysis.

## Series and Features

Any number of series can be created to run issue after issue. These aren't strictly news. But they're high interest, high readership items in any publication from *The New Yorker* to the organizational newsletter. It's always a good idea to include one or more to add variety to a publication.

A series needn't last forever. Set up and run a six, ten or twelve part series—whatever you have—identifying it as such with each issue. Readers gain a certain satisfaction from series. They like knowing something is going to be there, issue after issue, something with a predictable and comfortable familiarity.

*Highlight series.* Highlights of individuals or departments—employee-of-the-month, volunteer, or department head of the month—are gratifying to their subjects as well as interesting to other readers. Any organization with a good supply of interesting programs or products could run highlight series on them as a regular column.

*Profiles of executives.* Profiles of executive officers and board members acquaint employees with the individuals who set policy. They communicate something of why the organization is the way it is and where it is headed. Knowledge of what important people think creates a sense of identification, harmony and well-being among workers or members.

Profiles of important individuals outside the immediate organization—a powerful leader or expert in the same field, a politician committed to legislative changes that affect the industry, an influential individual who has frequent dealings with the organization, can be valuable aids to rank-and-file understanding of how the organization fits into the larger picture. Such stories flatter the individuals featured and build good will with them for the organization.

*History.* Reprints from old newsletters and annual reports and interviews with old-timers, retiring employees or founders can go into a series on the history of the organization.

One of the most popular columns in a large community hospital in San Francisco is a history column, written by a longtime staff physician, a descendant of some of the founders, who very much enjoys writing it.

History columns dramatize what it was like during crucial periods such as the great depression or World War II. They promote a sense of continuity and tradition in younger people and they build pride in the organization. Besides, they are fun to do.

*Inquiring photographer.* Not as widely used as it once was, probably because of increasing pressure for space for more legitimate news, is the inquiring photographer or "speak up" column. The usual form of this kind of column was to ask a question of four or five people scattered throughout the organization and run their answers to it along with their mug shots. A typical question might be: "What is your opinion of the flex time experiment being tried at XYZ Company?" The answers are kept short, usually only one to three short paragraphs. This kind of feature is useful in months when real news is scarce. Strive for lively questions, but clear them with key people first. Seek answers that show more than one side of an issue.

*Editorials and opinion columns.* This is the place for organizational propaganda. Contributed editorials and guest columns are clearly labeled as being from management or board members, executives or experts. Reprints of editorials from other publications are good sources, too, if they are relevant to your organization. The source should be asked for permission and given credit.

*Book reviews.* Reviews of books pertinent to an organization's activity are interesting to readers. If your circulation is big enough, most publishers will supply books and there are usually staff or members willing to review a book for the privilege of keeping it.

*Letters to the editor.* These columns are sometimes hard to get going, but they are valuable because they involve readers and make the newsletter in part really the readers'. Discreet editing helps keep the letters short.

Some letter columns evolve into advocacy forums where complaints, suggestions and ideas are aired between employees or members and management, but this role is usually limited to the insiders' newsletters only.

*Comics, cartoons, puzzles.* Regular features that give readers a laugh are always popular. The problem is finding a good, relevant source. Staff volunteer efforts may be relevant but unprofessional. Professional humorists may be masterful, but irrelevant. A specific cartoon by a major cartoonist may sometimes be reprinted with permission. Write for it. Syndicates sell humor features and puzzles and the like on a subscription basis. Check *Writer's Market* for listings under *Syndicates*, and write for samples and prices.

*Promotions.* Continuing update stories about the United Fund Drive, the blood bank or other civic efforts contribute to the success of those efforts and help the organization's image in the community.

If plant safety is an issue, run a regular item of "days without an accident" figures along with safety advice.

Firms in business to sell products are full of competitive salespeople who want to know how they measure up. Who's producing the most? Who's delivering the service that customers comment favorably on? How do they do it? How does the company compare with others selling similar products? What do *they* know that *we* don't know?

Pass around good ideas and techniques that the sales force uses. Let them contribute material for this column. Nothing succeeds like—or reads like—success!

*Feature stories.* Many of the ideas discussed here might properly be called features or special features and most could be developed as feature stories. *Feature story* is difficult to define because it means so many things. Generally, it connotes a story that is interesting for reasons other than its value as hard news. It is discussed in more detail in the next chapter.

## The Employee Publication

### *The Multiple Audience Dilemma*

Newsletter editors often face the dilemma of addressing more than one special interest audience at a time. The common interest of employees and outside readers may end with major news of the organization's progress. Then what?

If most of the readers of a newsletter are clients and other people outside the organization, news of the annual picnic, births and weddings, or minor staff changes are of little interest to the major readership and should be played down. But if most of the readers are employees, then such stories are appropriate, and are, in fact, what the readers want.

Serving an organization's employees is extremely important. They must not be ignored. Studies show that most employees judge their working places by their perception of top management, a perception gained primarily through the organizational newsletter.

Editors with large numbers of employee readers and outside readers often resolve this dilemma by publishing two newsletters—one for each audience.

In most cases, employees receive both publications, outside readers only the external publication. One Chicago agency alternates months, publishing an employee newsletter one month, an external newsletter the next. Other organizations print special inserts that go into employee copies of the external publication, but not into the other copies.

A common practice in many places is to publish a typewritten photocopied or quick-printed newsletter for employees each week or month, and a more elaborate typeset, printed monthly newsletter for a large outside audence.

Some large insurance companies and businesses put out a daily employee bulletin—one sheet, typewritten, with or without photographs, depending on the copying method.

## What Is News in Employee Publications?

If a publication is heavily employee oriented, or strictly for employees, these kinds of news items (in addition to those mentioned previously) are probably appropriate, and will have high readership:

- ☐ Sports scores of company teams
- ☐ Weather forecasts (in a daily)
- ☐ Features on outstanding or unusual employee hobbies, achievements, vacations
- ☐ Information about staff changes, benefit changes, etc.
- ☐ Health, nutrition, self-improvement columns

In a strictly employee or alumni publication, vital statistics are vitally interesting to readers: births, deaths, weddings.

Because people like to read about themselves and those they work with, there is a nearly unlimited source of feature story material at hand for the enterprising editor of an employee publication.

A company float trip or picnic can be covered as a feature story—complete with lively dialogue and colorful description of the surroundings. Or a story can be written with suspense and drama about the security officer who captured drug thieves in the hospital dispensary.

Stories about employees and their families' outstanding or unusual achievements and hobbies, vacations, and other leisure activities are well read in employee circles: Mike Jonas wins a citywide kite flying contest; Nelda Green's daughter, Tracy, wins a forestry scholarship to the state university; Joe Adamson catches the biggest channel cat anyone's seen in Rockaway County since '58; Marty Roberts has a fascinating collection of, would you believe, pigmy artifacts.

Features like these make the people—and the work along with them—seem less routine. They say, "We are interesting individuals in our own right—with lives and achievements worth noting."

## Finding the Right Tone

Many newsletters just grew, like Topsy, with the organization. As the organization got too big or employees too scattered to make communication by word of mouth, bulletin board and memo practical, a newsletter was started. More than likely, it was originally typed and mimeographed (and still might be), and contained a calendar of events, work schedules, meeting reports, information of this sort. Little by little, other news got into the newsletter and it began to fulfill the important function of keeping various segments of the organization in touch with each other.

Bulletin boards and monthly meetings may be effective, but a newsletter often becomes the principal means of communication between an organization's management and its employees. Good communication leads to other results. For instance, employee newsletters have been shown to increase productivity by boosting morale and by helping employees understand how their jobs fit into the overall company effort. Since it is so important, the employee newsletter should be approached intelligently and thoughtfully. *At the heart of the effective employee-oriented newsletter is the right editorial tone.*

If the newsletter assumes the stance of Pronouncement from on High, as the Official Voice of Management, its communications effectiveness is badly damaged. No one wants to be talked down or preached to, or told what to love.

On the other hand, if the newsletter relies solely on gossipy chit-chat, it doesn't provide real, substantive communication. Experienced editors of employee newsletters keep plenty of solid information coming at readers, and plenty of stories about the readers themselves.

Positive messages from management are presented matter-of-factly. It's unprofessional to "gush" in print. Negative messages from management are presented extremely low key—implied or presented subtly. An editor should never forget that a vital function of an employee newsletter is to improve employee morale.

A long-term series of studies has shown that almost *any* change in work environment increases productivity. The reason: people work better if they think that the people they work for are concerned about them. If management makes changes, employees feel their welfare is important. So if a newsletter can help effect needed changes in response to suggestions by employees, it contributes substantially to improving morale, and hence to efficiency and better production within the organization. Even if it doesn't effect the changes, it publicizes them, which is equally important.

A good job provides more than money. Some important job-satisfaction indicators are how important employees perceive their jobs to be, and how much individual recognition is given for the work they do. Stories explaining how a person's job is related to the overall success of the organization, and stories reporting outstanding work by employees or awards given for such work do much to help employee morale.

Equally important are stories pointing out company achievements or good deeds (civic contributions, foundation grants, etc.), stories that every employee can be proud of, and stories that demonstrate that employees are being fairly rewarded for their efforts.

A newsletter that accomplishes such goals as increasing productivity and improving morale and attitude in the working place is doing its job and doing it well.

## The Editor as Advocate

The professional newsletter editor is a hired gun, an advocate. You work for an organization; that organization pays you to represent them to the public. Your first duty is to the organization and its goals. (The volunteer editor is subject to the same expectations.)

So you pay attention to what the executive officers conceive to be in the best interest of the company, and work that vein of news.

This is not to say that you are a slave to the whims of anyone higher up the organizational ladder than you. Some of these characters get nervous, especially under pressure. Then they get bad ideas. No one gains personal respect, or respect for a publication or an organization, by complying with demands to print outrageous, misleading or false information.

When a publication loses its credibility, it loses everything. So, editors strive to strike a balance among loyalty to the organization, credibility to the audience, and personal integrity.

You can be firm, faithful to the facts, and fair, and still find a lot of room for advocacy within the confines of honest reporting. It all depends on what you choose to emphasize. You emphasize what makes the organization look good.

Even major newspapers, busily criticizing and exposing ills in the community, seldom criticize themselves. Newsmen on major dailies are sometimes asked to cover an insignificant or undesirable story because the publisher wants to promote some pet project. Worse, they are sometimes asked to ignore or slant stories—much more serious offenses for a publication purporting to serve the public than for a newsletter expected by its nature to advocate a particular point of view.

The great majority of newspapers, organizations, and companies as well, act in good faith. They try to do the right thing and do it well. They make mistakes, too. But an editor can help an organization grow stronger and better—in their own and in the public eye—by emphasizing what they do right.

For example, here's a story with great reader appeal: The consultants who just spent three years around the city planning office, drinking coffee, talking to secretaries, and spending $300,000 of taxpayer's money, *actually did nothing.*

Do you, the editor of the city hall newsletter, write the story and run it?

No.

Running that story would hurt your organization. So you ignore it, or better still, try to find *some* positive result to report, perhaps how the study is *expected* to save the taxpayers $4 million. If the local press gets the story and writes an expose, you are even more obliged to scare up a story showing any value that can be found in the study.

The newsletter, like the optimist, accentuates the positive and eliminates the negative. There are times, however, when the negative shouldn't be ignored.

If problems, complaints or rumors within an organization demand attention, the newsletter may be the place to resolve or clarify them. You can interview people about a problem and get different ideas of what should be done. Focusing attention on real rather than imagined issues may well work them out. Printing the truth behind a rumor often eliminates the rumor.

The newsletter editor who knows when to use news and when to ignore it, the firmly loyal and credible professional editor, is a valuable member of the organizational team.

# 4
# Write,
# Rewrite
# & Edit

# WRITE, REWRITE, AND EDIT

## Journalistic Objectivity

The newsletter editor, although an advocate, retains some professional journalistic objectivity without undue agonizing. Hard factual news is handled one way, interpretative features, another. Editorials are identified clearly as opinion material. So far so good.

Yet the editor's basic function is to exercise subjective judgment—which, while it is educated opinion, is still opinion. The editor decides which stories to run and which to drop. Judgment. The editor decides which words, sentences and paragraphs stay in stories, and which go. Judgment. The editor knows that the journalistic ideal of complete objectivity is just that—an ideal.

The editor who is also a news writer knows that *the best chance to approximate this much touted impartiality is in thorough news gathering, getting all sides—or as many sides as possible—of the story.* The honorable journalistic ideal of objectivity lives on in stories that are conscientiously researched and accurately reported.

This means gathering as much information for a story as time allows, through phone and leg work: interviewing principals, interviewing outsiders or the opposition, and searching through existing files and stories.

## Gathering News

News sources are myriad, but fall roughly into three categories:
1. Firsthand observation and interviews with principals.

2. What other people say.

3. Printed and other media stories, contemporary or historical.

Experienced reporters know that it's a good idea to get as much information as possible firsthand, by observation and interview of principal persons and events. They try to be where the action is, which, in the newsletter world, may mean something as seemingly unexciting as a committee meeting, speech, conference or groundbreaking ceremony.

But being there offers the opportunity to talk with participants, including those who deliver important reports or speeches. If something highly technical is involved, this is a chance to clarify the point so readers will understand what has actually happened. It's also a chance to enliven a story with quotes.

The alternative to being there, as the ads keep telling us, is using the telephone. Technicially, whenever you pick up the phone to ask someone a question about a story, you are conducting an interview. The telephone is valuable as a quick way to check facts and the spellings of names and to obtain additional information to round out a story. Of course, you can get an entire story via the telephone, and this is sometimes necessary if you are pressed for time or if the interviewee is far away. Whenever possible, however, it's preferable to interview news sources in person.

## The Interview

The interview, whether a quick one-question abbreviated one or a full-blown two-hour one, is a fact of life for writers and editors. A casual conversation with the boss at the water cooler about the implications of a memo on office dress code is an interview. A chance meeting with a fellow club member at the grocery can turn into an interview. It is good manners and good politics to let people know they're being interviewed in such chance encounters.

Any reluctance to interview news sources hampers the abilities of an otherwise good reporter. Yet, often writers don't want to do interviews. They're unsure of their ability to conduct a good one. Or they are afraid the person to be interviewed is "too busy" and will resent giving them time.

There is a way to overcome this reluctance. One way. The only way to master interviews is to do a lot of them. Interview people whenever possible. The more interviews, the more skillful the interviewer becomes.

And most people, no matter how busy or important they are, are flattered, secretly at least, that they are considered interesting enough to be interviewed. For a story about an important person, the interview is essential. There's no other way, really, to get the story. At least, there's no better way.

Some seasoned experts and celebrities will try to get the jump on you by attempting to conduct an interview by mail. They will ask for written questions and send back their written answers. The problem with this is simply that the questions are lifeless, and the answers will be lifeless. It's not a real interview. The result is an unsatisfying mixture of the too formal and the suspiciously phony. There's no satisfactory substitute for being there.

## Preparing Questions for the Interview

To be a successful interviewer, psych up for an interview. First, fix clearly in mind why this person is a good source—what he or she knows that the readers will want to know. What questions should you ask? The expert who can shed light on a subject that seems opaque to the average reader's mind may answer such a question as "What does 'creative financing' mean, exactly?"

The newly appointed president interests readers generally. They want to know all about him. Ask. "What are your strengths? Your weaknesses? What are your plans for the future of the organization?"

A highly paid consultant has just been hired. Rumors buzz. Readers want to know why she's worth her fee. "What previous projects have you done? What were the results?" Ask questions outright, even if you don't expect a straight answer. An elusive answer or no answer is still an answer—more than you get if you never ask. And such answers often reveal a lot.

## Homework

If you are hazy about what to ask the person to be interviewed, some homework is in order. Some basic background facts need to be ascertained. Who is this person, exactly? This is where other people and earlier news stories can help.

Ask other people who know about the interviewee; dig up previous stories from other publications. If the person is clearly representing one side of an issue, gather information presenting the other side.

The more sources and sides of an issue explored, the better the chance of getting information that will round out a good story.

Perhaps the subject of the story has come up before. Consult clips of previous stories.

## Files

Organized editors keep good files. Old newsletters and annual reports, memos, reports and clippings are kept in usable order. Good files are indispensable. They save time. They fill out stories that would otherwise be too sketchy or too obviously one-sided. They promote accuracy.

Functional filing systems employ simple, logical categories: names, subject matter, project or department titles, filed A-Z. Order and logic mean easy retrieval of information by anyone who needs to use the files. If they are skimpy or haphazard, or if they look like overstuffed chairs, they won't be used. Much time and energy is necessary to organize a workable filing system. But the time will be well spent, and the effort will pay for itself many times over.

A good filing system includes photographs of principal members of the organization who are often the subjects of newsletter stories. It includes photographs shot for use in previous publications, whether they were used or not.

Finding out all you can before an interview—through other people and sources—accomplishes two things. It enables you to better plan the range of questions to ask, and it eliminates the need for asking a lot of what the interviewee will justly perceive as dumb questions at the opening of the interview.

Nothing irritates an important person more than being asked things he prefers to believe everyone already knows about his stellar career. You can't open an interview with Jonas Salk by fixing on him with a pleasantly interested smile and asking what he does for a living.

## Conducting the Interview

Set a specific time for the interview. Allow time—probably at least an hour—to ask enough questions to adequately cover the subject, to over-cover it, really, because it's always better to have too much information than not enough.

Find out all you can before the interview. Then write down a list of questions. Many times, the person being interviewed will drift off the topic and into new, perhaps more interesting territory. That's all right. But there will be a lull, and that's when you can get back on track by consulting your list of questions.

Start out in a conversational way, without pad and pencil. The time to start taking notes is after you both are comfortable and the interview has more or less formally begun.

Good interviewers write fast, usually using a personal short-hand system. But beginners, and some experienced practitioners, may find a subject reeling off quote after quotable quote. If you just can't keep up, ask the subject to wait until you catch up. The subject is just as eager as you are to have quotes appear in print accurate and complete.

Another way around this problem is to use a tape recorder.

This is a simple solution, but like most simple solutions, it has drawbacks. One, the subject may not like to be taped. Two, it takes skill and luck to accurately record everything in a conversation, including gestures and throwaway phrases. And three, there's Murphy's law: anything that can go wrong will go wrong. There's always a good chance the recorder will malfunction and leave you high and dry and very embarrassed to ask for another interview.

Even if the recorder functions properly and every sound is captured, a taped interview can be time-consuming and inefficient. You must go back to the office, replay the tape, and then begin the painful process of extracting the important parts of the interview. Nothing is more frustrating than running a tape back and forth seeking that "great quote" you know is on there somewhere. By taping, you are *merely delaying the actual process of writing*.

Taking notes and running a tape may be the best policy. The writing is started, the high points are on paper, and the tape will serve as a back-up only, not as the principal source.

Type out notes as soon after the interview as possible. Rapidly scribbled words sometimes can't be recalled if too much time elapses between the writing and the typing of them. A single word on a note pad may stand for an entire sentence. Fill in the missing parts quickly or you will forget them.

## Writing the Interview Story

Writing the finished story from notes, you have two duties: (1) to be fair to the person interviewed and (2) to be considerate of the readers.

There will be a lot of repetition in any interview. Eliminate redundancies and repetition while running through notes seeking colorful and important quotes.

Similar quotes, or quotes on the same subject, may be widely separated in the interview. Pull them together to make the story more cohesive and easier for the reader to understand. Your obligation to the interviewee is not to say everything he said; it is to accurately represent what he said.

Where possible, paraphrase quotes into fewer, clearer words. Try to strike a happy balance between quoted material and paraphrase, without using too many paragraphs of either one all in a row. Alternate quotes and paraphrases.

Start paragraphs with a quote and follow with the attributive, "she said." Avoid starting with "Jones said that. . ." Tell the reader what Jones said, then that Jones said it.

Unless a quote is appropriate to key the reader to what the interview is about, a quote should not be used in the lead; a paraphrase is usually a better lead. But a good colorful quote is an ideal way to end a successful interview story.

## Approaches to Writing News Stories

### *Straight Reporting*

The most common approach to writing a news story is straight reporting. Immediately, in the first sentence or first few sentences, the writer tells the reader the most important part of the story, the part that makes it news.

Terrance McQueeny has been named president of *The Kansas City Star and Times*, replacing Michael Davies, who retired after 27 years with the firm. McQueeny has been with the *Star-Times* for 17 years, the past five as first vice president.

The following paragraphs expand and document the information in the lead.

The announcement was made following Tuesday's meeting of the *Star-Times* board of directors.

Davies, who is credited with building the *Star-Times* into a multinational conglomerate during his 11 years as president, had said six months ago that he would retire before the end of the year.

After being named president, McQueeny issued a statement saying that. . .

When all the essential information is on the page, the basic straight news story is complete. The story can stress any of the five Ws and H—*who, what, where, when, why* and *how*—though usually the *who* or *what* will be the most important.

## *Feature Treatment*

The alternative to reporting news straight is writing a feature story. But how do you know when you have a feature story on your hands? There are several characteristics to look for. The chief characteristic of the feature story is that although it has a news peg, it is not, strictly speaking, news.

A news peg is the justification for a story, the element that is news or has recently been news. In the example above, the news peg is that McQueeny is the new president of the company. A story about McQueeny's bike trip across the state with his son would be a feature.

What is played up in a feature story is not red hot news but some element certain to be of interest to most readers. That element can be celebrity status, humor, tragedy, suspense or an extraordinary event. A feature may be pegged on what the writer knows is of ongoing interest or concern to readers, something like the space shuttle or unemployment or inflation.

The feature element may be present in the kind of handling the story lends itself to. Is there a lot of highly descriptive and colorful material in the story? Is it rich in ideas or in historic background and significance? Then it's probably right for feature treatment. Another form of feature story is the analysis or explanation of a complex event, which helps readers to a more thorough understanding of a situation from which the hard news arose.

*Human interest.* Human interest stories are the most common of all feature story types. Their wide appeal is anchored firmly in most people's curiosity about other people's personal lives. Traditionally, such stories relate an exceptional event in the life of an average citizen: a good deed performed or experienced; a strange encounter, with a happy ending. But often now, these stories are based on lifestyle only: how people decorate their homes and themselves, how they vacation and exercise, what they eat. Properly handled, these stories are fine. Improperly handled, however, they go beyond curiosity to become tasteless and harmful *inhuman interest* stories that border on voyeurism.

*The time element.* Most newsletters are not issued daily; they come out weekly, monthly or even quarterly. Therefore the "news" in a newsletter is very likely the "olds." Events being reported may have happened two weeks, even two months ago.

Word of mouth, the daily newspaper, bulletin board announcements or memos have already delivered the essential facts to most readers. They know the story. The newsletter may very well be retelling it. What is the proper approach, then?

The newsletter story must restate the essential facts to clarify and record the known news. But, because most readers already know the facts, the newsletter writer undertakes to spark interest by presenting the story in a feature treatment.

For this reason, it is actually more difficult to write for a newsletter than for a daily newspaper. In traditional newspaper work, if not in most contemporary news reporting, if you gave "just the facts, ma'am," you'd done your work. Reporting known news takes some more work; it also often provides opportunities to exercise some imagination and show off some interpretive skills. Newsletters offer opportunities for features.

Features are often fun to do. Consider the life of the sports writer for an afternoon newspaper. He must write about a game that happened the night before and that was reported in the morning paper. Most readers know who won and what the essential plays of the game were. Does he hang his head over his typewriter because there is nothing left for him? He does not.

Everything else is left for him. And, you may have noticed, afternoon sports stories are almost invariably more interesting than their morning counterparts. An afternoon story may reveal the coach's magic (expletive deleted) words to the split end just before he went in to catch a pass for the winning touchdown. Or it may describe how a team achieved victory under unknown handicaps.

The news peg for the afternoon sports writer is still the game. But there is, as people say, more to the game than who won. There is how the game was played. And the feature story can explore that *how* in detail, at some leisure. *Time is actually on the side of the feature story.*

*The delayed lead.* Feature stories usually take a delayed lead; that is, the facts of the story are not given right off. They are worked into the story, but the focus is on some detail or idea that is not the hard news focus. A feature story is to reporting what a close-up is to photography. The writer selects a certain element from the big picture and is able to give it a closer, more thorough and thoughtful look. A strong writer with an eye for detail thrives on this style of reporting.

One word of caution, however. A writer of limited gifts and skills may find that feature writing brings out the worst in him or her and may delay the lead until no reader can find it. If you are not sure of your skills, approach feature writing very gingerly, a little at a time, practicing and learning as you go what readers do and do not like.

## The Essential Stylebook

Every publication requires rules, commonly understood and written rules. A stylebook contains such rules for consistent style and usage. In any given publication, capitalization, for example, should be consistent. A publication that prints *Vice President* on one page and *vice president* on the next leads astute readers to suspect that such untidiness may extend to larger matters. If the writers cannot pay attention to such little details, then can they be trusted to get other things right, like the facts? In publishing, small inconsistencies affect credibility, even as in the society at large a sloppy person's appearance affects his or her acceptance by some fastidious citizens.

A stylebook can include as few or as many rules as you think necessary. Some, e.g., the *University of Chicago Stylebook*, are several hundred pages long. The Associated Press and United Press International stylebooks, used by many newspapers, are much shorter.

A model stylebook is given in the appendix to this book. It is brief, and it is offered to suggest what topics to consider in making decisions about your newsletter style. Readers will disagree with some of its directives. That's all right. Usage standards vary and are open to argument. But within any organization that publishes material, a guide to consistent usage is needed for all writers. A stylebook will prevent time loss to constant decision-making while writing. It will prevent time loss when a writer and an editor get into an argument over the appropriateness of semicolons for separating items in a series.

Some of the conventions covered in the stylebook in the appendix are those for capitalization, punctuation, grammar, spelling, abbreviation and numbers. Conventions for abbreviations and numbers are especially troublesome.

Will you and other writers for your newsletter abbreviate state names in the old way, as Ariz., Calif., Miss., and Tenn.? Or will you use the postal service abbreviations AZ, CA, MS and TN? Either is acceptable, but a decision on one for consistent use is mandatory.

Should dates be abbreviated as in Jan. 6? Or do you prefer January 6? Decide.

In which usages will numbers be spelled out and in which will they be written as numerals? Will it be ten or 10? One million or 1,000,000? Fourteenth Street or 14th Street? Decide. Decide in all the cases of usage you can think of, and then write down the others as they come up and you make rulings on them.

Will a person's title and surname be used in second reference (Mr. Abernathy, Ms. Lewes)? Or will only the surname be used (Abernathy, Lewes)? This has been an unsettled issue lately and has taken some entertaining forms. One major daily got into terrible trouble with its readers when it printed a story about a convicted murderer, referring to him respectfully throughout the story by the title "Mr." After the outcry, the newspaper ceased to extend courtesy titles to murderers. Then Shana Alexander wrote a book about Jean Harris, the very ladylike woman who murdered Herman Tarnower, the doctor of Scarsdale diet fame. When the newspaper printed a review of the book, they referred throughout to "Ms. Alexander" and to "Harris."

Usage that involves a controversial issue may take some time to resolve. Should a female chairman be a chairwoman? A chair? Must men then be chairs too? This sometimes gets absurd. But these issues must be conscientiously faced and worked out. And then a decision must be made so that you can get on with the work at hand, which is to get the newsletter out.

When the basic decisions are made and circulated in writing, a stylesheet has been born. It will grow into a stylebook in its own time as controversies and questions arise and are resolved. Write decisions down the minute they are made, to avoid any future confusion.

Begin a list of words that cause recurrent trouble, whether with their spelling or their use. If "comprise" is given on your list as meaning what the whole does to the parts, never again does a writer on your staff spend ten minutes agonizing over whether the states comprise the Union or the Union comprises the states.

In short, having a stylebook means never having to say you're stymied by something stupidly small.

An agreed-upon dictionary, to be used as the final authority in usage, should be made available to all writers. *Webster's New World Dictionary* is the choice of many major dailies.

## Elements of News Writing

Good writing employs proper grammar and usage. It is clear, easy to read, and easy to understand. Good news writing has these features and several other distinguishing characteristics. They are as follows:

### *Accuracy in Facts and Spirit*

Make every effort not only to establish the veracity of all information in a story, but also to assure that the total effect of the story is not misleading.

Check names and addresses carefully, using standard references such as telephone books, city directories and file clippings. Much information comes secondhand from newspapers and other media. Such data should be checked against basic sources. The more sources used, the greater the chance for accuracy.

When checking via telephone, exercise special care, because of the chance of misunderstanding. The letters *f* and *s*, for instance, sound similar. Ask that names be spelled out, using a verification system: *A as in Able, B as in Baker,* etc.

If you are still uncertain of a specific fact after checking more than one source, qualify the statement: *It is believed that. . .* (or) *Jones said he understood that. . .*

Even when you have verified all specific data, it is still possible to give the reader a false impression. Omission of one side of an issue or of an essential background fact can distort a story. Inadvertent comment and vague usage alike can mislead the reader. How old is an *elderly* man? A *young* one? Be specific.

Attribution of an emotional attitude to a person being quoted is another problem. Words like "demands," "denies," or "denounces" have strong meanings and they attribute strong feelings to the speaker. "Said" is safe and neutral. There is nothing wrong with using it repeatedly. Avoid choosing strong words only for the sake of variation or color. Choose them only if they are the right words.

Be careful of assumptions and conclusions. If they are someone else's, attribute them. State the facts accurately and let readers draw their own conclusions.

## Short Sentences and Paragraphs

News writing serves the reader who is in a hurry. The reader wants the facts: specific places, names, numbers, dates and events. The extra adjective or adverb is out of place in news writing. As a rule, limit sentences to fewer than 10 to 20 words and to *one* idea. Use active, not passive voice because active voice is concise and vigorous. Write that Elton Jones made the motion, not that the motion was made by Elton Jones.

A good length for a paragraph is two or three sentences, which is not what you learned in freshman English. But the object of an essay written in an English class is to develop a theme or an idea thoroughly. The object of news writing is to get the news to readers. Long paragraphs set in type in a narrow newsletter column would seem impenetrable to the reader. They are, in fact, difficult to read. Keep them short and simple.

Another virtue of short paragraphs is their flexibility. Often new information must be added to a story after it is typeset, or part of the story must be cut to make the story fit available space. A story constructed of short paragraphs makes either of these tasks easier to do without rewriting whole paragraphs.

## Short Phrases and Words

Tell the story in the fewest words possible. It's harder to write, but easier to read. Look for unnecessary words in circumlocutions like the following.

| | |
|---|---|
| arrived at the conclusion | concluded |
| at the present time *or* at this point in time | now |
| drew to a close | ended |
| for a period of | for *or* during |
| for the purpose of | for |
| gave its approval | approved |
| held a discussion | discussed |
| in order to | to |
| in the area *or* field of | in |
| in the immediate vicinity | near |
| in the majority of cases | usually |
| in the near future | soon |
| made arrangements | arranged |
| put in an appearance | appeared |
| reached an agreement | agreed |
| with the exception of | except |

Avoid cliches, bromides and trite expressions. The list is long and constantly expanding.

All-out effort, better half, bigger and better, blessing in disguise, cool as a cucumber, crying need, few and far between, hangs in the balance, heart of the business district, hopefully, in the limelight, Lady Luck, last but not least, loomed on the horizon, meaningful, Mother Nature, Mr. Average Citizen, nipped in the bud, no uncertain terms, picture of health, sign of the times, silver lining, view with alarm, whole new ball game.

Circumlocutions can always be reduced to more direct statements. Many phrases can be replaced by a single word. Reduce them, replace them.

## Defined Acronyms

Newsletters for scientific organizations and bureaucracies abound with acronyms and abbreviations: HUD, HSA, EPA.

The reader has a right to know what they mean. On first reference, spell them out: Department of Housing and Urban Development, Health Systems Agency, Environmental Protection Agency. On second reference, refer to them as *the department* or *the agency*, unless there is more than one department or agency mentioned in the story.

## Specific Usage

Use definite, concrete, descriptive words. *The event was not held because of unfavorable conditions* is nonspecific. It could mean any number of things. *The picnic was cancelled because of rain* is specific; it says exactly what it means.

## Right Words

Right words are usually the obvious ones, but it's always good to look a word up in the dictionary to verify that it means what you think it does. The model stylebook in the appendix contains a section on often misused words.

A thesaurus is useful in providing the word you seek but can't quite utter into speech. The minute you see it you recognize it as *the word.* Using a thesaurus on a crazed quest for fancy ways to say plain things, however, is often a "search and destroy" mission. The search for swell-sounding words may yield them—but the words may be the wrong ones and may destroy meaning. The operation is a success, but the patient has died.

Unless you are familiar with a word found in the thesaurus, check it in a dictionary for exact meaning before putting it on the page. Errors made with the aid of a thesaurus are commonly ludicrous and sometimes legally dangerous. Saying that a combative councilman was "truculent" may seem a good idea at the time. But it will seem a very bad idea when the word is read by someone who knows its meaning—the councilman, for instance. He may not like to be thought of as "savage and cruel."

## Writing Good Leads

The first part of a story—the first few sentences or paragraphs—is the *lead*, pronounced *leed*. It must do its job or the reader will turn to another story.

The writer's job is to capture the reader's attention, to state essentially what the story is about, and to be interesting enough that the reader wants to read on.

The notes for a story will contain the answers to the questions *who, what, why, where, when* and *how.*

As you look at these six elements in your notes, you will assess their importance to your particular audience in terms of (1) timeliness, (2) proximity, (3) consequence, (4) prominence, (5) conflict and (6) oddity.

Decide if your notes contain a single most important news element or if there are several that are of nearly equal importance.

As you weigh these factors, keep in mind that *where* and *when* are seldom of top importance, though they can, indeed, sometimes be the most newsworthy element. (The accident happened on the way to the wedding. The baby was born in a pool hall.)

*Why*, i.e., the cause, reason or purpose, and *how*, i.e., the means by which, will sometimes be the most interesting point.

But usually, the *what* or the *who* is the real news of the story. The *who* is almost always newsworthy in a small circulation newsletter whose readers know everyone in the organization and like to read about them. The important part of the story will sometimes be a combination of these two—*who* did *what* or *what* happened to *whom.*

The trick to good lead writing is to immediately focus on this most newsworthy point of the story and to reserve other details until later in the story. Try to reduce the essence of the news to a single sentence or even a single word.

Try this simple device. Pretend you are calling a friend to report the news. You might start: "Do you know what happened?" "No, what happened?" Your answer to that question, "The board just voted to give us a 15 percent travel allowance increase," is your lead, essentially. At least it is the lead content.

Once you have decided what information should go into the lead, it still must be written in the most attention-getting way possible. Is there an especially interesting or unusual way to phrase the information? Is there a colorful word that can be put into the lead? Is there a dramatic or humorous element to the story?

The lead takes two basic forms: the *direct lead* and the *delayed lead.*

The direct lead conveys immediacy and gets right to the point. It can touch on a single news element, combine two news elements or summarize several elements such as the results of a meeting. It is important to avoid putting too much in the lead. Do not confuse the reader with too much information all at once.

Here is a snappy single-point lead:

Local bicyclists will ride more safely on our streets starting today, thanks to a new bikeway system just approved by the city council.

Here is a lead burdened with too much information:

George Burns, Mary McCleary and Robert Day, members of our congregation, all suffered minor injuries when the car they share in a car pool skidded on ice as they were driving to church and collided with a car driven by Ruth Ann Schull at 10th and Washington Streets shortly before 11 a.m. Sunday, according to Sheriff Mike Kindinger.

Documentation, clarification, authority and additional details can be saved for the paragraphs following the lead. In the example here the essential news is that three church members who shared rides were injured on their way to church. Other information should be delayed until the paragraphs following the lead.

The delayed lead takes a more roundabout approach than the

direct lead. It uses several sentences to set up a background or explain the context for a reflective mood story. It employs suspense to capture the readers' attention and then leads them to the newsworthy outcome.

Delayed leads start with a teaser, an interesting side issue, and then work to the central news point. They arouse anticipation rather than thrusting the news straight at the reader.

Like all municipal officials, Mayor Terry Wood of Outback, Mo. is faced with a tight budget.

And like other officials, he needs to meet the demands of the citizens of his community for services like park and street maintenance. To do so, he needs, among other things, a pickup truck. But money for a truck is not in the Outback budget.

So the mayor called the Mid-America Regional Council, which coordinates the distribution of excess government property for the region. Staff members checked a catalog issued monthly by the state and found a 1966 Dodge cargo pickup truck listed. The truck was located at the Defense Property Disposal Office in Columbus, Ohio.

Forms were filled out, and soon the truck belonged to Outback.

The only hitch: Wood had to pick it up and drive it back to Outback.

In the past six months, MARC has helped distribute $350,000 worth of equipment. . .

The story goes on to list equipment distributed, and it ends with the two oddest requests—for a railroad locomotive and some baseball equipment.

For both direct and delayed leads, every conceivable rhetorical device has been used: contrast, question, literary allusion, parody, quotation, dialogue, figurative speech, direct address, epigram, and description.

Any number of different leads could properly be used on the same story. With experience, writers quickly find the right opening. When a lead feels right, a story will sometimes unfold easily, telling itself the rest of the way.

A good lead catches the reader's attention, whether the story is long or short, straight news or feature, analysis or background.

## Writing the Body

### Short Items and Stories

For very short stories, the body may be a single sentence or paragraph documenting the lead. A surprise punch ending is effective in short shorts.

> A new membership directory has been published for members of the American Rural Electric Association (*the lead*). It is available for the asking from the national office; write or call for your copy (*the body*).

> Jim Garrity, who chaired the committee that planned the annual company picnic last month, anticipated every problem except one (*the lead*). He broke his leg the day before the picnic and was unable to attend (*the body*).

Short shorts come in handy. They enable an editor to cover a large amount of news in brief form. The same is true for the reader. Short shorts are much in demand when an editor begins laying out pages; they fill small holes in the page and, when boxed with a rule, enhance typography.

### Longer News Stories

The body of the traditional longer news story usually takes one of three forms: (1) inverted pyramid, (2) chronological, or (3) structured.

*Inverted pyramid.* The inverted pyramid form requires a writer to confine separate blocks of information to paragraphs; these paragraphs are arranged by importance, the most important early in the story, the least important toward the end.

Readers get the most important information first and can stop reading when they have learned as much as they want to know, before the end of the story. Furthermore, in making up a page using stories written in this form, the editor can drop paragraphs from the bottom to make copy that is too long fit the space available, knowing that essential information will not be lost.

*Chronological.* Organizing a story chronologically is not only natural for the writer to write, it is natural for the reader to read. After the lead, which focuses the reader's attention, the writer merely tells the rest of the story in the sequence in which the events happened. Art imitates nature in the very simplest way in chronological writing.

*Structured.* The structured form, as a rule, builds to a climax, keeping the reader in suspense. It captures the reader's attention, intertwines documentation, authority and facts throughout the body, and leads the reader to a conclusion, often with a twist or surprise ending. It cannot be cut indiscriminately without leaving the reader hanging.

## The Two-Story Story

Sometimes it is difficult to weave in important collateral information with the main news thread of a story. One device is to write two stories—the main news story and a *sidebar*, a second story containing the related information. This not only leaves the two separate-but-closely-related stories clear and direct, but also brightens up a page layout of otherwise "gray" text.

Frequently the second, sidebar story is an illustrative feature on the same subject as a general news story. For example, if a record heat wave is the subject of a general news story, then a feature sidebar might contain a story of how one resourceful person is fighting off the heat. Another use is to break out statistics from a main story that is heavily laden with numbers, and run them in a table in a box adjacent to the story.

## Rewriting a Story

The first draft of a story is seldom the best. There are holes to be filled, authority to be added, wording to be improved, and meaning to be clarified.

Read the first draft. Have someone else read it. Make corrections, compare it with notes, look for ways to sharpen, brighten and improve the story. Check facts, shorten sentences, remove unnecessary and inaccurate qualifiers, rewrite phrases and sentences.

Check spelling and punctuation against the stylebook. Recheck names, addresses and figures. Make sure that facts are documented and authorities are given.

Look at the lead. Does it contain enough information? Is too much crammed into it?

Read the draft out loud. It's easy to skip obvious errors when reading silently. A sentence may look all right but, when read aloud, not read smoothly and logically. If a sentence or phrase isn't clear, rephrase it.

## Credibility

A publication's credibility depends on accuracy, fairness, and consistency. Each issue, each story, affects credibility. Note significant errors in one issue and print corrections in the next. Establish a reputation as a conscientious editor.

Be alert to the special credibility problem of newsletters: stories that seem to issue from on high, that carry no attribution, even for very opinionated material. "Who," the reader will ask, "says so?" The reader has a right to know not only the facts and opinions themselves, but also who is stating them.

Some editors believe that to avoid controversy and ignore adverse opinion is to protect the organization. But such a policy may, in fact, hurt credibility. Often, a controversy met head on, in print, with fair representation of all sides, can be honorably resolved. Ignoring criticism won't make it go away. Take the opportunity to present your side of the issue and to put it in the best possible light. Negative gossip and criticism spread quite naturally all by themselves. Use the newsletter to present the positive side. Demonstrate that there is nothing to hide, that your group is doing what it sincerely believes is right.

## Legal Considerations

The First Amendment to the U.S. Constitution guarantees freedom of speech and press. But this is a *qualified* freedom, preceded by obligations. Freedom of speech is limited by laws pertaining to libel, privacy and copyright.

### *Libel*

Newsletter editors seldom venture into the dangerous journalistic waters of reporting trials, criminal activities, or politics. Still, many libel suits spring from innocent mistakes such as mistaken identification or misplaced photographs, and you need at least a working knowledge of what these laws are about, because they can affect you just as they affect editors of national periodicals.

A libel has four elements:

(1) A defamatory statement. That's a statement that "holds a person up to public ridicule, contempt or hatred, causes him to be shunned or avoided, hurts his reputation, damages his credit, or injures him in his business or profession."

(2) The statement must be published. Publication can be by words, pictures or other means, and courts have held that a statement is published if only one person other than the writer and victim sees it.

(3) The victim must be identified. Even if his or her name doesn't appear in print, it is enough if the reader can infer who is meant.

(4) There must be injury. But the law holds certain statements automatically injurious: those imputing a crime, low moral character, a loathsome disease, or insanity.

The law of libel is different in each of the 50 states, but these are the essential elements in all of them.

In all states, anyone connected with a libel may be sued, but as a practical matter, the victim usually sues whoever has the money—in the present case, your organization.

Victims who win libel suits may collect general damages (whatever a judge or jury considers reasonable), special damages (actual monetary loss), and punitive damages (if they can show malice).

There are three basic defenses for the publishers:

(1) Proving the *truth* of the statement and the *absence of malice.*

(2) *Proving that there was a qualified privilege* to print the information (e.g., from an official court record).

(3) Proving that there was a *right of fair comment*, applicable in criticizing any work of art (e.g., a play or a book) that has been offered for public approval.

A published retraction of a statement or photo that attracts the accusation of libel is not a defense but will show good intent and help reduce damages.

Strive for truth and accuracy in reporting. If you venture into controversial areas, say a lawsuit in which the organization is involved, exercise special care. Consult the company lawyer and clear what you write *before* it is published.

## Privacy

The right of privacy is a person's right to be left alone. This law is vague and varies from state to state. But several points are clear and are pertinent to the newsletter editor.

(1) Anything newsworthy that happens in public can be reported.

(2) A public figure loses some claim to privacy.

(3) The right to privacy ends when a person consents to publication. Consent is implied if he or she agrees to an interview.

(4) A person's name or photograph can't be used for monetary gain without his or her consent. Get a release.

(5) Truth is not a defense.

## Copyright

The 1978 copyright law allows a person to copyright original works of literature, art, music, etc., for his or her lifetime plus 50 years.

Facts or news cannot be copyrighted, but the actual wording of an account of those facts can be. Writers drawing from copyrighted material may paraphrase it, and the convention is to give credit to the copyright holder.

Work done for the federal government cannot be copyrighted. This law permits free use of the oceans of material prepared by government agencies.

If an employee creates a "work for hire," e.g., for an employer, the employer is considered the author and may obtain a copyright on the work unless there has been an expressly written agreement between the two specifying otherwise.

## Shield Laws

Most states have shield laws, laws protecting reporters from naming the source of information; but these laws limit this protection to employees of the news media and exclude newsletter writers and free-lancers.

## Elements of Editing

On large newspapers, completed stories go to managing editors, news editors, telegraph editors and city editors who judge them for relative news value. The editors decide how long to run stories, what headlines to put on them, what typographical treatment they will get, and where they will go in the paper. Stories are then funneled to a copy desk where copy editors carry out directions. There are editors all over the place.

But on smaller publications, there is often only one editor to perform all these functions.

Good editing can make the difference between a poor newsletter and an acceptable one, between an acceptable publication and a good one. Here's how to approach the task of thorough editing.

### Copy Editing

When you go over a story, you will be doing many jobs at the same time:

1. Read a story through quickly, sizing it up for content and relative news value.

2. Correct obvious errors of fact or spelling.

3. Check the story for conformity to stylebook rules.

4. Decide if the story is too long for its relative news worth and if so, trim it. If it's incomplete or too skimpy for the import of the news it has to tell, round it out or, if possible, have the original writer do so.

5. Go over the story carefully, looking for mistakes in punctuation and grammar and facts. Recheck facts, especially names, addresses, numbers and titles.

6. Watch for potentially libelous statements; make sure the story is accurate and that it represents fairly all sides of an issue.

7. Write the headline.

As you polish the story, look for the elements of good news writing: conciseness, clarity, accuracy and vigor.

Cut unnecessary words and phrases, tighten loose writing, rephrase jumbled or confused sentence structure, substitute virile verbs for limp ones, change the general to the specific.

Look for hidden leads. Is the real news buried? If so, pull it up and write a new lead.

Do not make changes, however, for no reason. It is not enough that you would have written the story differently than the writer did. Preserve the special approach and flavor of the writer's style.

This, basically, is what a copy editor does. But the news writer-copy editor-editor often has a special problem. You may have written many of the stories yourself.

Editing your own copy is risky. You are apt to overlook the mistakes you made when you wrote it. It is difficult to see the story from a new perspective. Let some time elapse before you edit your own stories, so that they won't be so close. Tackle them with the critical eye and objectivity you would use on other writers' stories. Be tough on your work.

But if possible, avoid editing your own stories. Perhaps there are others on your staff who can edit your stories. If you are a one-person operation, turn elsewhere for help. A top secretary could proofread your story for grammar, punctuation and spelling. An executive in another department could check it for facts and overall content.

And there is nothing wrong with having the source of a story check it for accuracy. Make it clear in advance, however, that you don't want the story rewritten in some ponderous, non-news style, that you want it read only for overall accuracy.

Find the most talented editing help you can. Even among trained journalists, really top copy editors are hard to find. Ideally, they are knowledgeable, skeptical, principled, irreverent, artistic and talented. They have a sense of humor, take the job seriously, and do not make changes for the sake of change. Yet they take nothing for granted. They question facts, names and grammar—and they check them against references: dictionary, telephone book, city directory, world almanac, stylebook, and grammar.

Copy editors keep the spirit of the story, but at the same time they organize, brighten, correct and polish it. They leave a story much better than they find it.

# 5
# Headlines

# HEADLINES

## The Importance of Headlines

Nothing distinguishes a professional newsletter from an amateur one so quickly as the quality of the headlines. Because headlines are prominent, the reader's eye goes to them first, and in the first few seconds of scanning, the reader's crucial first impression of the publication is formed. The importance of taking the time and effort to write good headlines cannot be overstated.

## Writing Good Headlines

Well-written headlines distill the essence of the news point of a story. They are positive and specific; they contain strong active verbs and short simple words.

Writing good headlines takes practice and study. Spend some time with a good newspaper, studying the headlines in it. Headline writers on large newspapers are often among the most talented and experienced people on the staff. They become specialists in headline writing because they have a seasoned, almost instinctive understanding of the essence of a news story. They write headlines hour after hour, day after day; and, for this reason, they excel at writing headlines.

In contemporary headline writing, unfortunately, there is a trend toward the "cute" headline. Puns are widely used by formerly staid newspapers. Some of the uses are better than others. Typical examples of this breed of humorous headline are the following: **Bjorn Again!** (when Bjorn Borg won a tennis tournament) and **State money woes/Give hospital pain** (on a general news story).

So many major metropolitan dailies use puns so relentlessly in headlines now that one suspects something is up, that their market research divisions have announced that puns sell papers. However, some great newspapers that, as of this writing, do not use puns in headlines are *The New York Times*, *The Washington Post*, and *The Philadelphia Bulletin*.

In addition to studying professionally written headlines, spend some time learning the classic journalistic rules for writing good ones. Review these rules (see *How To Write a Good Headline* below) before each headline writing session.

## What a Good Headline Does

*Gets attention.* The first function of a good headline is to get the reader's attention. That's why it is printed in larger type than the text. Even editors of typewritten newsletters use typeset headlines or headlines produced with rub-on type. If this is not possible, they use a larger typing element. They achieve a boldface effect by typing a headline twice, the second time inserting an index card between the paper and the typewriter platen.

*Tells the story.* A good headline tells readers what a story is about. It induces them to read the story. Even if they don't, however, they can catch the essence of a story from a well-written headline. Readers should be able to pick up the main news in a newsletter by scanning only its headlines.

*Leads the reader into the story.* Successful headlines do more than tell the story. They capture the readers' interest and make them want to read on.

*Classifies the story.* The size and style of a headline give readers some idea of the importance of the story. They show the relation of the story to others in the newsletter. The bigger the head and the more prominence it is given on a page, the more important the story.

*Enhances the page.* The typography and style of a headline work to enhance the appearance of a page. Headlines work together on a page to present a lively and interesting face, to form attractive patterns as well as to tell the news.

## What a Headline Says

The headline is often taken from the lead. The main news in a properly written straight news story is in the lead, which may run for several sentences or even several paragraphs. The headline writer sifts through them, pinpoints the news, and forms a story sentence—a sentence that sums up the main news point of the story.

Say the story is about the hiring of five new teachers by a school district for the coming year. The story sentence would be: school district hires five new teachers for 1983-84 term. The headline would feature the key words of that sentence: five teachers hired.

Then, depending on the amount of space allotted for the head, it would include such other information as the term they were hired for, and who hired them. This kind of headline is relatively easy to write.

A story that comprises various facts may need a general headline. Say an agency has reorganized. It previously was divided into five departments. One new department has been added and two of the former five departments have merged.

The main news point is not that a new department has been added or that two other departments have been combined. The main news point is that there has been a major reorganization.

To single out only one of the points would not tell the whole story. The headline writer would focus on the reorganization and its expected result.

## How Headlines Fail

Many newsletter headlines not only fail to focus on the main news point but also rely on words too general or too vague to give the reader the gist of the story. There are several categories of headlines to avoid.

*The label head.* A company forms a bowling league. The headline reads: **Bowling League.** Bowling League what? Readers, if they have the time and patience, must read the story to find that a new league was formed or that they are being urged to join it. The headline, at the very least, should tell readers that.

*The question head.* Another kind of head that falls short of doing its job is the question head: **Is the Transit Plan Working?** Readers may be interested enough to read the story to find out the answer. But the headline space could be better used to tell readers why the plan is working or why it isn't.

*The vague head.* Another failed headline is the "meeting held" variety. The headline **Committee Meets** tells readers next to nothing. What did the committee do? What's the news?

*The how or why head.* The *how* or *why* headline is a little better: **How Stock Options Work.** This at least holds out a promise to readers and may even tempt them to read the story. But it communicates no concrete information.

*The clever head.* A clever headline may work for some feature stories—those that involve humor, suspense or extraordinary events or that are highly descriptive. But a good clever headline is more than just clever; it captures what any good news headline does: key words, color, vitality, specific images, and the essential news.

Alliteration, puns and rhymes seldom work the way you want

them to. If you suspect that a headline employing one of these conventions will evoke groans rather than smiles from your newsletter audience, rewrite it in a more conventional form. Occasionally allusion, irony, wit, metaphors, catch phrases, labels, questions and captions work in feature headlines, although they do not work in straight news headlines. It is all right to break the rules and try one of these devices occasionally for a feature story.

Good headlines, whether on straight news or features, bring focus to a story and announce it with flair and action.

## How To Write a Good Headline

1. *Use active voice.* The dynamic active voice saves words. **Man Bites Dog** is livelier than **Dog Is Bitten By Man.** The subject and verb act as one. Also, the passive voice costs extra words and often makes a headline too long to fit the space available for it. Use the passive voice, however, if the active voice will delay the essential news. **Pay Hike OKd By Board** puts the core news first. **Board OKs Pay Hike** delays the news.

2. *Use present tense.* To convey a feeling of immediacy, write headlines in the present tense, even if the story reports something that happened in the recent past. Write **Robber Flees** rather than **Robber Fled.** Use the infinitive or future tense to announce a future event. **Lawyers To Debate Insanity Plea.**

3. *Use short, pithy words.* Use short synonyms for long words. *Panel* or *group* will more likely fit into a headline than will *committee.* Furthermore, long words can obscure meaning. **Work Begins On Broadway Bridge** communicates more than does **Bridge Repair Plan Implemented.** Adjectives are seldom needed in headlines, and there is seldom room for them.

4. *Avoid to be verbs.* Headline writers delete helping verbs such as *is* and *are.* This omission saves space and punches up the headline. **Physicians Asked To Staff Clinic** omits the understood helping verb *are.*

5. *Make positive statements.* State negative information in

positive form. **No Action Taken On Ruling By Pacifists** would be better written **Pacifists Decline to Act on Ruling.** This construction also avoids confusion about who made the ruling. The pacifists did not make the ruling, yet the first headline makes it appear that they did.

6. *Be specific.* Use precise words. **Editor Named Employee-of-the-Month** communicates a more concrete idea than does **Woman Named Employee-of-the-Month.** If readers know the editor, write **Janis Wright Named Employee-of-the-Month.** Likewise, write **Wagoner Wins Design Award** rather than **He Wins Design Award.** Headlines that name a person work especially well with a photo of the person.

General words and vague words make dull headlines. One of the deadest headlines is the *standing head,* the "Message from the President" label headline that appears over a regular column. Write a live headline about the president's message; tell readers what the president has on his or her mind this week. Then maybe they'll read the column.

Being specific does not include putting insignificant or out-dated matter in a headline. The specific date, for instance, does not matter much after an event. Don't cause confusion by using a past date in a headline. The reader's first response is to think he or she has missed something.

7. *Be accurate.* A headline that sums up a speech must include attribution. Don't write **Inflation Rate To Slow Down** as though it were a fact. Part of the news is who says so. Write **Inflation Will Slow, Kemp Says.**

8. *Be impartial.* Watch words that color a headline's meaning or reflect the writer's opinion. Words like *denies* or *claims* have connotations that may misrepresent the facts. **Rose Lashes Board's Action** may overstate Rose's criticism.

9. *Don't repeat key words.* **Committee Ousts Committee Chairman** is unacceptable. Look for synonyms; find another way to phrase the headline. **Committee Ousts Its Chairman.**

10. *Avoid confusing line-divisions.* Don't divide hyphenated

words or words that go together from one line to the next. **Group Votes To/Renew Plea.** Here the split infinitive can be avoided by reworking the head: **Group Votes/To Renew Plea.**

11. *Omit articles.* Generally, the articles "a," "an"and "the" are omitted to improve action and to save words.

12. *Avoid abbreviations.* **Salesman Wins Trip To LV.** Readers may not catch on that LV is Las Vegas.

13. *Avoid excessive punctuation.* Use semicolons instead of periods, single quotes instead of double; use commas sparingly. The comma is often used in place of *and* in headlines.

14. *Use important numbers only.* Except for one, numbers in headlines should be written as numerals: **23 Leave Camp for Wilderness.** Dollar amounts are often meaningless unless they are compared to other figures: **$100,000 Added to Cost of Bridge** may be insignificant if the bridge costs $4 million, or it may be important if the bridge costs $200,000.

15. *Avoid contrived headlines.* Puns, rhymes, and alliteration are seldom appropriate in headlines.

## Establishing Headline Styles

When the time comes to lay out the newsletter pages, you will need to have a few standard sizes and styles for headlines, for the sake of consistency and readability. Pick a few type sizes and styles, and plan to write all headlines to conform to one of those styles. Limit the number of typefaces to two or three. Use conventional type sizes—30, 24, 18 and 14.

Because one important function of headlines is to classify news value, the basic principal in establishing headline styles is to provide consistent identification of the importance and the character of various stories.

A model headline schedule is given in Appendix 2 of this book. The schedule you make up should include at least four basic headline styles. Slight variations on these basic styles will round out the total of your standard headline styles.

## Four Basic Styles

1. *Large bold headlines for top stories.* These headlines run across the top of an entire page, or two-thirds of it or half of it, depending on how big you want your biggest headlines to be.

2. *Secondary headlines.* These are smaller and/or lighter than the number one headlines. They will go with stories of secondary importance, usually shorter than the major stories.

3. *Heads for special stories.* These variety headlines will go with features or items that are not straight news. They may be used with rules or boxes for emphasis and design interest on a page layout.

4. *Heads for short news items.* These headlines usually run one column wide on short short news stories, those about one to three paragraphs long.

Experiment with different typefaces and type styles. Try boldface and italic. Try the same headline written in different patterns on the page. Write it all one one line; then try the same headline written on two or three lines. Try different widths, across one, two or three columns.

Try some headlines with a *kicker,* a line written in smaller, lighter type than the main headline and run above it. The smaller line might be in *italic.* Try a *hammerhead,* in which the top line is in larger type and the second line is in the smaller. Try a *deck* headline, one with two or three smaller, lighter lines of type under two or three lines in larger, bolder type.

Working with published examples will give you a proper feel for headline types and uses. Study those given in the model headline schedule of this book. Study those used in newspapers, how they look and when and where they are used.

You will notice that very few headlines are set in all capital letters. Many headline writers capitalize the first letter of each word except for prepositions and articles, to emphasize key news words. But the trend now is to use the same capitalization rules in headlines that are used in writing sentences.

Develop a schedule that suits your newsletter style and subject matter. Study the model headline schedule in Appendix 2 for sample styles of the four categories listed above. If you are a newcomer to news editing, you probably have not even thought about the notion that headlines must fit a space, rather than vice versa, but they must.

## Making Headlines Fit

No matter how well a headline tells the story, no matter how attractive it is, it must fit the space available for it. The writer who is also the editor and pasteup artist has the apparent advantage of being able to alter layout to fit the headline. But it is better to avoid this temptation: inconsistency and sloppiness of appearance are a sure result of such a practice. Such lack of discipline is one of the leading causes of ugliness in amateur newsletters.

If a headline is only slightly too long for the space, you may ask the typesetter to "*kern* the head," that is, to squeeze the letters together slightly. Or, since most typesetters can set any type size from 5½-point to 72-point, you could ask to have the type size dropped a point or two. But, again, too much of this kind of practice will produce erratic pages.

Once you have a model headline schedule, write headlines to fit into one of the styles you have established. To fit headlines, you must face the tedious task of counting them.

How do you count a headline? You must count the characters, which means any letter, number or other symbol. Characters are counted in units.

Can you just count each letter and other symbol as one unit? If you type your newsletter on a typewriter that gives equal space (one unit) to each letter, you can. If you type it on a proportional spacing typewriter or if it is typeset, you cannot. Typeset letters are proportionally spaced. Thus letters occupy widely different spaces on the page:

ffff
MMMM
iiii
mmmm
jjjj

The width of a character varies from typeface to typeface, but generally you can rely on the following unit counts.

Count as one-half unit the letters *f, l, i, t, r,* and *j,* the capital *I,* punctuation marks, and the spaces between words.

Count as one-and-one-half units the *m* and *w,* all capital letters except *M* and *W,* numbers except for *1,* and the symbols such as the $.

Count all other lower case letters and the number *1* as one unit.

Count the capitals *M* and *W* as two units.

Most typesetters will give you a pica chart that lists the exact width of each character in the typefaces you use.

To fit the headline, first estimate its length by counting each letter as one unit. When it is about the right length, go back and compute the actual total count. After you've written and counted many headlines, you will develop a feeling for how many words go into a line. The task of counting headlines thus becomes much easier with practice. Here is a basic sample of a counted head:

| B | i | k | e | | R | o | u | t | e | | S | t | u | d | y | |
|---|---|---|---|---|---|---|---|---|---|---|---|---|---|---|---|---|
| 1½ | ½ | 1 | 1 | ½ | 1½ | 1 | 1 | ½ | 1 | ½ | 1½ | 1 | 1 | 1 | 1 | 15 |

| T | o | | B | e | | C | o | n | s | i | d | e | r | e | d | |
|---|---|---|---|---|---|---|---|---|---|---|---|---|---|---|---|---|
| 1½ | 1 | ½ | 1½ | 1 | ½ | 1½ | 1 | 1 | 1 | ½ | 1 | 1 | ½ | 1 | 1 | 15½ |

When you have used a headline such as the one above in a newsletter, note the count, enter that information along with the headline into your headline schedule file. Later, when you choose a similar head for a story, you will know how it looks and what the approximate count will be.

Although it is not necessary that a head completely fill a line, especially when the headline is *flush left*, i.e., lined up with the left margin, a headline should come within three units of filling a line.

Headlines with gaping holes look unprofessional and ragged. Usually the writer could have filled the unused space with more information.

A good list of short headline words is available in the book *Headlines and Deadlines* by Robert E. Garst and Theodore M. Bernstein. Such a list provides short synonyms for long words and is a valuable tool for making headlines fit.

# 6
# Format
# & Makeup

# FORMAT AND MAKEUP

## Readability and the Right "Look"

To get the news you have so carefully gathered and written onto the page and out to readers, you must decide what form it will take. The paper the newsletter is printed on, the typefaces it is written in, the kinds of photographs and other graphics that will illustrate it—all are part of the format, and all must be carefully chosen both for readability and for the right "look."

## Paper

To assure optimum readability and to show off photos to their best advantage, choose a white or light-colored paper. Dark papers can turn words into mush, photos into mud. Choose a paper of medium weight, one that will not allow the ink to bleed through and show up on the other side of the page. This is especially distressing if the newspaper is printed on two sides.

Many newsletters and small newspapers are printed on 22x35-inch paper and folded to eight letter-sized 8½x11-inch pages. This is a good format because it is simple to handle and very economical. Odd sizes and odd folds can attract attention, and some are very attractive, but they may confuse the reader or divert attention from the news content. And they can be expensive.

Paper choice also depends on other considerations such as the need for flexibility and the image you want to convey to readers. If you are bent on presenting an odd or unique image to readers, use odd or unique paper or folds.

If the amount of news available for each issue varies, use a flexible format—perhaps one 11x17-inch page folded once. This yields a four-page newsletter of two pages printed on two sides, and during months when there is more news than usual, you can simply insert an extra 8½x11-inch sheet to carry it.

If you use photographs and other illustrations, either of the standard formats described above will allow plenty of flexibility for working with them. If you do not use photos and graphics, you may want to stay with a literal, old-fashioned news *letter* form, using as many 8½x11-inch sheets as required for each issue. This is the size used for most newsletters reproduced at an "instant print" shop or photocopied on office equipment.

Your printer can supply paper at a reasonable cost. If you want to buy paper yourself, however, from a supply store, check to be sure it will fit on your printer's equipment and that it is of the right weight and quality for the job. Explore the possibilities of various paper sizes and weights, and talk to a printer about the best paper for the best price.

## Typography

If you typewrite a newsletter on a standard typewriter, you have only one typeface, and that is that. If you use a typewriter with multiple fonts, you have a variety of typefaces from which to choose two or three for text copy. You can buy large, headline-style type in the form of *rub-on* or *press type*, available in alphabet sheets from art supply stores. Such type is rubbed or pressed onto the page, letter by letter.

If you use typesetting, there are literally thousands of typefaces to choose from. A newsletter can be set in one typeface throughout. Single subject newsletters such as Kiplinger's and other brief financial letters, as well as any true letter-style newsletter, may be printed in one typeface. This appropriately gives a sense of immediacy to the news.

But in most newsletters that bring private news and announcements to a specific audience as infrequently as once every two to eight weeks, one typeface can get boring.

For variety, use two or three good solid faces. Roughly their uses will be these: one main typeface to be used in hard news stories, another to be used in feature stories and lighter items, and a third face for use on special items such as calendars and announcements.

Additionally, you will need two or three larger, bolder faces for use in headlines. The choices are basically ones of size and style.

### *Type Sizes*

Type sizes are stated in units of measurement called points.

    1 point  =  1/72 inch
    12 points  =  1 pica
    6 picas  =  inch

The sizes of type you choose will be determined primarily by the age of your audience. When choosing faces for the text of stories, readability is the most important consideration. Readability studies have shown that at different ages, people prefer different type sizes.

# This 24-point type is a good text size for preschool children.

## This 18-point type is a good text size for children ages five to seven.

This 14-point type is a good text size for eight- to nine-year-old children.

This 12-point type is a good text size for children ages 10 to 12 and for adults.

This 10-point size is widely used in texts, apparently for very keen-sighted older children and younger adults.

Remember, too, that this cycle ends as it begins. If most of your readers are 65 and over, it's back to the big typefaces. Large-print books for older persons and persons with certain visual limitations are set in 14-point and 18-point type. Even many legally "blind" people can read very large type such as this 18-point type.

For headline type, use faces that harmonize with the faces used in the text. Choose clear, clean faces and use them in reasonable sizes, e.g., in 14- to 30-point sizes on a standard 8½x11-inch page. Anything larger will look zany; anything smaller will be too nearly the size of the body text to achieve proper headline emphasis.

### Type Styles

Having considered sizes, choose some styles. Typeface design styles fall into five general categories: roman, italic, script, gothic and display.

*Roman* describes the general family of typefaces used in the text of almost everything you read, including what you are reading now. *Roman* loosely denotes a standard typeface whose letters are straight up and down; that is, the vertical lines of the letters form a right angle to the horizontal line of the page.

There are hundreds of different designs of roman typefaces. This book is set in one called *Goudy Old Style*.

Within a given design, many variations are available: regular, italic, bold, bold italic:

*This is Goudy Old Style italic.*

**This is Goudy Old Style bold.**

***This is Goudy Old Style bold italic.***

Each of these variations is also called a typeface. So, the word *typeface* means two things: the whole design family—*Goudy Old Style* is a typeface—and the specific style or form of that design—*Goudy Old Style italic* is a typeface. A type *font* describes both specific style and size: 12-point *Goudy Old Style italic* is a font.

*Italic faces slant to the right. They are generally used to emphasize words and passages, and they are often used in* figure legends, captions *and* cutlines, *i.e., the copy that accompanies and describes a photograph or a technical illustration. Do not set long passages in italic.*

*Script type is intended to imitate handwriting and is therefore used only when you wish to convey intimacy. Use it in announcements and invitations. Do not use it for general news.*

GOTHIC TYPEFACES BASICALLY HAVE LINES OF UNIFORM THICKNESS AND NO SERIFS. THEY CAN BE USED BOLDFACE IN HEADLINES. THEY ARE NOT APPROPRIATE FOR GENERAL NEWS COPY.

**Display type, larger, heavier and more ornate than text type, is used sparingly, as a design element, chiefly in publication titles.**

All typefaces are either *serif* or *sans serif*. The letters in a serif typeface have small extra strokes at the ends of the lines that form the letters. This Goudy Old Style is a serif typeface.

Within serif faces, the *old styles* have slanted serifs; *modern* faces have straight serifs.

Now look closely at this *Helvetica,* a sans serif typeface. You will see that every letter in it is made of an unadorned straight or curved line. Many people dote on sans serif typefaces, regarding them as elegant, spare and clean, which they are. There is no controversy about their usefulness in headlines and other short lines of type. They are ideal for such uses. But there is great controversy about their readability in long passages of type. The present writers are of the opinion that sans serif faces should *not* be used for long texts. Our rule is: Do not ever use sans serif typefaces for a full-length news or feature story.

Many readability studies support the opinion that serif typefaces are easier to read. When one newspaper, the old *New York World Journal Tribune,* switched from a sans serif to a serif typeface, its circulation increased. So did the morale of its staff.

It is thought that the reason for the better readability of serif typefaces is that the serifs give readers added clues to quickly distinguish letters. The letters—and words—do not all look so much alike. We find sans serif type in large doses generally harsh, boring and wearing on the eye.

One other factor to remember is that one typeface will appear larger than another typeface of the same point size. The reason for this is that type is measured from the top of *ascenders* on letters such as *d, l* and *k* to the bottom of *descenders* on letters such as *j, y, p* and *g.* An *ascender* is the part of a letter that extends above the body of the letter; a *descender* is the part that extends below it. Short letters, like the lower-case *x,* have neither ascenders nor descenders. Typefaces with short ascenders and descenders have a larger *x-height,* i.e., the height of the lower case *x.* The larger the x-height, the larger the typeface looks on the page.

Choose typefaces and sizes that will not distract the reader from the news content. Avoid typefaces that are too bold and fat or too light and thin. Avoid ones that are too condensed or extended. Avoid all elaborate typefaces for use in news text copy. If, when you are looking through a typeface book, a typeface catches your eye—and you find youself saying something like, "Oh, isn't that interesting!"—don't choose that typeface for news text. It may, however, be all right for some headlines.

Choose clear, readable roman typefaces for text, ones that convey a sensible, professional image and that are the right size for your readers. Choose headline typefaces that emphasize the text and enhance the page.

## Column Width and Margin

The width of a column of type affects text readability. The wider the column, the larger the type should be, and the more white space (called *leading*—rhymes with *wedding*) you need between the lines. Long lines of type set right on top of one another are hard to read; the eye loses track, trying to get from one line to the next. Narrow columns (22 to 30 picas wide) usually require an extra point of leading between the lines. Wider columns are more readable if two or three extra points of leading are allowed between lines. (See *How to Mark Specifications, p. 93.*)

The general rule is that column width should not be less than 13 times the type point size, or more than 30 times the type point size. Taking the eight-and-one-half-inch-wide page of most newsletters as an example, each column in a two-column layout set in 9-point type would be about 3.5 inches wide. If you use three columns, they will each be about 2.5 inches wide. This is an estimate. The exact width of columns will depend on how much space you leave for margins and between columns.

## Readability Table

| Type (Point Size) | Minimum Column Width | | | Maximum Column Width | | |
|---|---|---|---|---|---|---|
| | Points | Picas | Inches | Points | Picas | Inches |
| 8 | 104 | 8.6 | 1.4 | 240 | 20 | 3.3 |
| 9 | 117 | 9.7 | 1.6 | 270 | 22.5 | 3.7 |
| 10 | 130 | 10.8 | 1.8 | 300 | 25 | 4.1 |
| 11 | 143 | 11.9 | 1.9 | 330 | 27.5 | 4.5 |
| 12 | 156 | 13.0 | 2.1 | 360 | 30 | 5.0 |

Columns should be separated vertically by at least six points (one-half pica). If they are set closer together than that, a rule should separate columns. Maximum space between columns can vary. The primary consideration is to achieve an attractive, readable page.

The range of readable column widths for typewritten pages can be determined from the readability table. An *elite* typewriter produces the equivalent of 10-point type. A *pica* typewriter produces the equivalent of 12-point type. The minimum column widths for typewritten newsletters, then, would be 1.8 inches for *elite* type and 2.1 inches for *pica* type. The maximum column widths are 4.1 and 5 inches, respectively.

Allowing for margins, a newsletter that is typed across an eight-and-one-half-inch page has a column width (line length) of seven inches—too long for good readability. Break the page into two columns. This will not only make the news more readable, it will open up new layout possibilities.

Another consideration in column choice is whether to set the columns with *justified* or *unjustified* margins. A justified margin is one in which every line ends at the same place. Thus, you can lay a ruler along the right edge of a column of justified type, and each line will meet it. An unjustified or *ragged right* margin means that some lines will be a few units shorter than others.

Newsletters printed from typewritten copy look fine with ragged right margins. The time it takes to justify margins on an ordinary typewriter is really not worth the end result. Even with a typewriter that will justify the margins for you, the resulting lines may contain odd spaces between words. This is jarring to the eye and can distract the reader from story content.

There is a trend toward the use of the ragged right margin, because it is freer, more natural, and less formal than the justified margin. Some studies suggest that it is more readable, too.

## How To Mark Specifications

Typesetters working with copy that is not clearly marked with specifications (i.e., not "specked") have two alternatives: to hold up the work until you can be reached or to use imagination to determine your wishes. The first practice causes work to stop; the second may result in copy having to be reset. Both cost time and money.

Consult your typesetter about available typefaces and the sizes and styles considered appropriate for newsletter stories and headlines.

Specify the following information by writing it on each story:

(1) The width of the column in picas. Use no fractions except one-half, e.g., *30 pi, 22½ pi*.

(2) Kind and size of type. Use the complete name abbreviated, e.g., *12 pt Bodini reg roman; 10 pt Bodini light ital; 14 pt Caledonia reg roman; 18 pt Goudy bold*.

(3) Leading space. The space between the lines is called *leading*. Standard leading for 10-point type is 10 or 11 points. (The leading space includes the space taken up by the type. Therefore the leading size will always be as big as or bigger than the type point size.) Specify *10/12 Goudy Old Style*, and the copy will be set in 10-point type with two points of extra space between each line. Specify *10/11* and the copy will have one point of extra space between lines. Specify *10/10* or do not specify leading at all, and there will be no extra space between the lines. This type you are reading now is set 12/14.

(4) If a passage is to be set in all capital letters, write *all caps*. If

it is to be set upper and lower case, write *c/lc* or *u/lc.*

(5) Paragraph indention size. Paragraphs are usually idented one *em*—i.e., the amount of space an M occupies in a given typeface—for columns up to 21 picas wide, two ems for wider columns. If you do not want paragraphs indented, write *no indent* or use the flush left bracket symbol [. *See Copy Editing Marks and Typesetting Specifications*, Appendix 5.

## Elements of Makeup

How all the elements are put together on a page constitutes *makeup*. The constituent elements of the private newspaper or newsletter are, roughly, these: text, headlines, photographs and other illustrations, design amenities, masthead, nameplate, and other special elements used in every issue.

### Text

The single most important element in page makeup is the text of the stories. Everything else on the page is there to enhance the text. Your group's news is, after all, the reason for having your own private newspaper.

The text will be of several kinds: hard news stories, feature stories, and short items and announcements. If you want variety of typography to enhance interest on the page, use two or three typefaces on the three kinds of text.

### Headlines

Headlines announce the stories, set the tone of the page. They are an important page design element. They make the reader want to read on, or they herald such an onslaught of boredom that readers instinctively know to read no more. Headlines are so important in news presentation that we have devoted an entire chapter to them. (See Chapter 5.)

## Photographs

If your format allows photographs, they can add great interest to stories, to pages. They lend reality to words, make permanent the images of important people, events and things in the world shared by your readers.

Photos must be clear and in focus, and they must add information or interest to the story they accompany. Never use a bad picture, i.e., one that is fuzzy or shot from so far away that it shows essentially nothing. Use only crisp black and white photos, and try to get photographers to approach subjects with some imagination.

Nothing is more boring than a newspaper filled with pictures of groups standing in rows, two men shaking hands and exchanging checks and documents, and lifeless mug shots. Try to get some life in photos: people walking, talking, doing something; buildings or outdoor spaces in interesting light or from unusual angles.

A note of warning: Don't rush out and buy expensive equipment that no one can handle. Get a volunteer or professional freelance photographer, or get a good basic 35mm camera that you or someone else can use easily. Don't spend hundreds or thousands of dollars on long lenses and pink filters until someone can use the basic camera competently.

Whether you shoot photos yourself or assign them, look for interest, action, dramatic tension, character. Suggest the following as goals for photographers.

*Action.* Capture an animated moment in a candid shot. For action, sometimes a photo is deliberately blurred slightly, to represent rapid motion.

*Angle.* Look for unusual angles to represent a fresh viewpoint. Even for something as stolid as a building, a photographer can climb to a high spot or lie down to get a dramatic angle.

*Comparison/Contrast.* In group shots, the relative importance of group members can be expressed in unusual or striking arrangements with one person front and center and subordinate members in the background.

To show something extremely small or large, use contrast. For example, a tiny computer chip could be photographed on a thumbnail to show its size relative to that of something the reader is familiar with.

*Composition.* Compose photographs to show a strong central point of interest. Some shots can be framed in foreground elements such as fence slats, tree branches, doorways.

*Character.* For individual portraits of story subjects, also called *mug shots*, take a lot of both candid and formal poses, searching for unique qualities in the character of the subject. Don't insist that subjects stare motionlessly into the camera. Let him or her talk and even move around a bit, and catch the moment when an attitude is struck.

Most photos are improved by *cropping*, i.e., trimming off irrelevant elements or blank spaces. Cropping is a final form of composition. Look for the main point of the picture and decide what can be cut to emphasize it.

Vary sizes and shapes of photos used in page makeup. Don't hesitate to use long, narrow pictures if the subject matter lends itself to that treatment.

Photographs are often run too small in newsletters. Find the space to give good photos adequate play. Vary the sizes of photos on one page. Find the most important one and run it larger than the others. Strive for variety and emphasis.

Another note of warning: Do not run photos of yourself in your newsletter. The only exception is if you are new on the staff or are leaving and it is routine policy to run mug shots on these occasions. Never, for any reason, run more than one photograph of yourself in an issue. If you show up in the background in a good annual meeting or picnic photo, that's all right, but do not feature yourself in such photos. Amateur editors are often tempted to use the newsletter as a showcase for themselves; professional editors are seldom so tempted.

Printers can *scale*, i.e., enlarge or reduce photos to fill a space of the same proportions on the page. The space a 5x7-inch photograph will occupy can be just about any size from 2½x3½ inches to 8x10 inches. Using a pocket calculator or a proportion wheel (available at graphic supply stores), you can determine the final size yourself. Or, establish a space of the same proportions (height to width) of the photo, and then ask the printer to reduce or enlarge the photo to fill that space.

## *Captions*

Give special attention to the *caption* or *cutline* on a photo, i.e., the text that accompanies and describes what is in a photo. Be sure it identifies all people shown and that it does not announce what is obvious: "This is a cow." "Shown here receiving. . ." "Pictured here giving. . ."

Stress the story behind the photo. With a simple mug shot, add a quote or a teaser line: *Moses Campbell. . .a winning idea.*

Add and explain significant facts that can't be ascertained from the photograph. If a sign is shown in a foreign language, translate the sign message in the cutline.

Captions can be enhanced by the use of a small *kicker*, i.e., a short headline above the caption, or by putting the first couple of words of the caption in heavier type such as boldface or boldface caps.

It is believed that headlines run above a photo are lost on the reader, who will see the picture first and then go right on reading down the page and on to other things.

## Graphic Iillustrations

Use drawings, sketches and clip-art as they are available and appropriate to the quality and tone of the image you want the newsletter to project. Books of such clip-art may be purchased at art supply stores. Or write Dover Publications, 180 Varick Street, New York, New York 11014 for their free catalog of very inexpensive books of clip-art and design elements such as borders.

## Design Amenities

Pages can be enlivened with such design elements as screens to make part of a black and white page a light gray, or with lines, borders, boxes, and so on. Your printer can help you with things like screens. Art supply stores have books with decorative design elements that can be applied directly to pages. Or write Dover, mentioned above.

## Name and Nameplate

The name of a newsletter conveys the nature of the organization or subject matter it covers. Strive for more flair than naming yours "The (Your Group Name) Newsletter." But avoid the too cute or the too obscure name. Christen your newsletter with accuracy, liveliness and good taste.

Have a professional designer design the nameplate or title logo that will identify your publication to readers. The *nameplate* is the name of the newsletter or newspaper in large, perhaps display type, plus any other design elements; it usually runs entirely across the top of the first page. The nameplate makes a first impression and a continuing one because it appears on every issue.

The nameplate, also called the *flag*, can be located in different places from issue to issue, if you want the variety or need the flexibility. If you do, make up one that runs all the way across the page, another that goes half across, another that runs down the vertical line of the page.

## Masthead

Newsletters with second-class mailing permits are required to run an identification statement in the first five pages, telling the name of the publisher, address, frequency of issue, issue and volume numbers, date, post office where postage is paid, and subscription price.

All newsletters should run a masthead containing at least the organization name and address and, if it is not obvious, a short statement of the publication's purpose. This information can go on the nameplate or the masthead. But the names of the editors and the officers of the publishing organization go on the masthead, not the nameplate. For example: *The Boston Cyclist: News of recreation and transportation cycling in Eastern Massachusetts. Published by the Boston Cycle Club, 10 South Street, Boston 02341* can go on either the nameplate or the masthead or both. But the names of the officers and editors go only on the masthead.

Like the nameplate, the masthead can be made up in two or three different shapes and sizes to accommodate different page layouts. The masthead is usually shaped more or less like a box and is often boxed in with lines, while a nameplate is more like a flag, often waving across the top of the front page.

## Mailing Space

Newsletters that are mailed as self-mailers, i.e., without envelopes, must carry a mailing space and a stamp or postal service bulk-rate mailing permit indicia, as well as a place to put the reader's name and address. This space is conventionally the bottom one-third of the last page of the publication. Nothing says it has to be there. But it should be incorporated into the format in such a way that it does not interfere with reader interest. Check current postal regulations for the dimensions of the space required.

## Calendar

A regular calendar of events is the heart of many newsletters and is regarded by many readers as the most important information in it. Use some design elements to brighten up a calendar, but never emphasize design over readability. Calendars, like maps and charts, often do best on an outside page of a publication.

## Putting it all together

When all the elements that will make up an issue are gathered, they must be made to fit onto the pages and to do so in proper relation to one another. What story goes where? What size should photos and headlines be with various stories? What can be done to break up large, dull areas of nothing but type? Preliminary decisions about these matters are made by fitting the copy into a *dummy*, i.e., a pattern for the final product.

## Copyfitting

How much space do you have in the newsletter for layout? Calculate the number of *column inches* by multiplying the length of one column times the number of columns on a page, times the number of pages in the newsletter. Say your newsletter is four pages (two 8½x11 sheets printed on both sides) in a three-column format. Then—allowing for one-inch margins at the top and bottom of each page—you have three 9-inch columns, or 27 column inches per page, and 108 column inches per issue.

Final copy is typed or typeset into the column width you have chosen: about two inches wide in a three-column layout on an

8½x11 page, or three inches wide in a two-column layout on an 8½x11 page. Measure to see how many column inches of written copy you have in these columns.

Remember that everything—all graphics and photos, nameplate, masthead, mailing indicia and space (if the publication is a self-mailer), and headlines must come out of the total column-inch measure. So, by the time you have made space for all of them, and depending on how much white space you use, you may want only about 60 to 80 column inches of written material for a 108-column-inch newsletter. If you have 102 column inches of written copy, plus photos and graphics, something is going to get squeezed. You will have to start editing in earnest: cutting out copy, reducing photos, making headlines shorter. Plan ahead.

## Dummying

*Dummying* is making a pattern for an issue. First make a list of all the stories to go into an issue. Indicate how long they will be when typeset. Rate them by importance. Note those that have photos with them and list other photos that will stand alone.

List other material to go into the newsletter—calendars, nameplates, mastheads, mailing space, graphics and illustrations.

Decide what size columns you will use.

Typewritten newsletters are often written clear across the page, although they would look better and work better with a two-column layout, each column about 3.5 inches wide, with a one-third inch *gutter*, i.e., white space, between the columns.

Editors of typeset newsletters normally use two or three columns on a page, sometimes, though very rarely, four. (Be sure to use a smaller size type for four columns or there will be too many gaps between words and too many hyphenated words.) You can use a combination: one wide column of say 28 picas, and a narrower column of 16 picas; or two columns of perhaps 16 picas and one narrow column of 10 or 11 picas.

At first, it's easier to use the same format for each issue, the same number of columns throughout the newsletter or at least on each page. But as you gain experience, it's desirable to strive for variety to make pages more interesting.

Calculate how much space all this material will fill. Calculate how much will go on a page. Sketch out dummies of pages. A blank dummy page will look like this:

## DUMMY LAYOUT

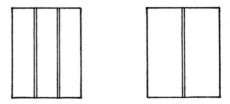

Now arrange the material on the pages. The most important story, of course, will go on page one. Other stories with high priorities will go to the last page and to page 3. Some pictures will go to the tops or bottoms of pages opposite the one the story they illustrate is on. Assign other material such as mastheads, calendars, etc. to key parts of pages, usually top or bottom, striving for balance and symmetry.

For instance, a picture at one corner of a page can balance a masthead at the other corner. Compare facing pages: Do they work together? That's how a reader will see them.

Stories of secondary importance go lower on pages. Assign headlines to stories, using a variety of styles and sizes that will at once reflect the importance of a story and blend with other heads on the page. Don't put two identical style heads side by side; they cancel each other out.

## Jumped Stories

Extra long stories may have to be *jumped*; i.e., continued on another page. Avoid this if possible because readers tend to quit reading rather than turn the page. But sometimes jumps are necessary.

When a story is jumped from one page to another be sure to end with a *jump line*, "*continued on page 5*," and when the reader goes to page 5 be sure there is another jump line, "*continued from page 1.*"

Put *jump headlines* on the continuation of stories inside. A jump head can be the same as the headline on the front page, or a similarly worded head, possibly of a different size. The jump head can be merely a key word from the original head. If the original head is *Olympic Athletes To Be Tested for Drug Use*, the jump head could be *Athletes/Drug Use* or *Drug Use* or *Drugs*. Use anything that will direct the reader to the remainder of the story.

If possible, break a jumped story in the middle of a sentence. This will induce the reader to turn the page to finish the sentence at least, and perhaps the story.

Use an index on the front page to call attention to a story inside. If you have extra space on the front page, use a *solo* , i.e, a one-line head, at the top or the bottom or in a box in the middle to call attention to an important inside story.

There is no set sequence in which an editor accomplishes all these steps in dummying. Some work a page at a time; some work on all the pages at once. Experience will teach which works best for you.

To make a final, more exact dummy, make two photocopies of all type, photos, headlines and other material. One set should be carefully proofread. The other is cut up to make the dummy. Using the rough sketch dummy as a guide, cut out stories and tape them into position. Modify your layout to accommodate larger- or smaller-than-expected stories.

When the dummy pasteup is completed, make another

photocopy of each page to doublecheck overall appearance. At this stage, your layout is substantially complete. The photocopies will be used as a guide for final pasteup. Correction of errors discovered during proofreading can be pasted over the typeset errors on final pasteup.

## Text Breakers

Several graphic techniques can break up *gray* text on a page, i.e., lines and lines of type without visual interest. Boxes and rules can be used both on headlines and on textual matter.

Paragraphs can be separated, with extra white space between them. Beginnings of each paragraph should be indented. Indents are usually one *em*, the space occupied by the capital letter M.

Other techniques for breaking up the text are *subheads*, i.e., two- or three-word phrases set in boldface calling attention to some fact coming up in the next paragraph:

. . .mining products, chemicals and grain.

**The Next Phase**
The second phase of the study, now underway, will identify feasible opportunities for port use.

Or put the first two or three words in boldface caps every few paragraphs:

. . .commuting through heavy traffic to reach the airports from these areas.

***The update recommends*** that a new west airport be built by 1985 to serve those portions of the two counties.

Or set an occasional paragraph in boldface or italic. Large capital initial letters can be used to start a story or to break up text. These can be set above the line or inset into the text.

T here are two universal problems in a disaster, according to Don Milsap of the Kansas City, KS.- Wyandotte County Civil Defence Office. The first problem is communication. The second is that no one...

Short stories can be boxed for emphasis or to liven up a dull spot on a page.

Occasionally, a story can be screened so that a fine shaded tint box covers the story. Don't make screens too dark. A 10 percent screen is usually enough. Consult your printer about screening.

> This is a 10 percent screen

Another typographical brightener is reverse type, i.e., white letters on black for headlines. Don't overdo it.

Extract dramatic quotes or statements from stories; set them in a different typeface, and run them boxed in the text. This breaks up large areas of gray and induces the reader to read a story.

Once you have prepared all the material for your newsletter, painstakingly proofread the text for errors, and prepared the dummies, you are ready for final pasteup.

# 7
# Production
# and Distribution

# PRODUCTION AND DISTRIBUTION

## Pasteup

Professional pasteup artists charge by the hour or the page. Some are better than others. If your budget will allow it, and if the only alternative is to do it yourself, there are several advantages to using a professional.

They use their own equipment and supplies, which relieves you of this expense. They are familiar with printing requirements and can eliminate possible later problems at the printers. Given a good dummy, they can work fast.

There are disadvantages, too. Besides the extra cost, one major disadvantage is loss of control. The layout artist works at home or office, and you cannot be physically present to answer questions, suggest needed modifications or revisions, or check pasteup as it progresses.

Furthermore, the pasteup artist may not be familiar with your organization and cannot be expected to monitor content—an artist works with form. Mark clearly which heads go with which stories, which cutlines with which photographs. These are frequent sources of error.

If you do pasteup yourself or get a volunteer to do it, you will need certain equipment.

Basic tools for pasteup include an X-acto knife with a supply of blades (No. 16 blades work best), scissors, a metal straight edge rule with pica markings, a transparent plastic ruler with alignment marks, a T-square, a 30-60 triangle with inset edges, a layout board, rubber cement or wax, grid pasteup paper, and a burnishing roller.

You do not need an elaborate drafting board. Small, low-priced layout boards work fine. (One place these are available is Dot Pasteup Supply, Box 369, Omaha, Nebraska 68101).

Use rubber cement or wax. Other kinds of glue make paper wrinkle. If you use rubber cement, get the large bottles with adjustable length brushes, so just the tip of the brush touches the cement. Use thinner. Rubber cement gets gummy and hard to work with.

Professionals use an expensive machine to put a thin coating of wax on the back of copy to be pasted down. Small, inexpensive models (about $20) are available. Waxed copy has the advantage of being easy to move; it's easier to pick up or reposition than copy stuck with rubber cement. One disadvantage is that small corrections sometimes fall off.

Buy professional pasteup boards with grid squares printed in *non-repro blue*, i.e., blue ink that will not show up when copies of the page are printed. Or make up your own pasteup board, with columns marked, and have your printer run off a quantity of them.

Indicate margins and column widths with non-repro blue lines. Cut out copy and headlines. To position headlines, draw a light blue guideline through the middle of the characters or under them; extend the lines at either side, to match them up with the layout guidelines.

If you are using a light table, the blue grid lines of the pasteup board will be your layout guides. Make sure lines of copy run straight across a page, not at an angle.

Cut copy to fit. If the leading is consistent throughout a story, equal-size columns should contain the same number of lines. If you have an odd number of lines, the extra white space can be distributed in the white space between paragraphs, usually in the first of two columns.

When cutting copy, leave plenty of paper at the edge of each copy block. That way you can handle copy by the edges to avoid getting smudges on the copy itself. Cleanliness is essential at every stage of pasteup. Keep a couple of rags handy, one for wiping your fingers, the other for gently wiping the face of the copy after it's pasted up.

After columns of type and headlines are aligned, put a sheet of paper over it, and run a burnishing roller over it, pressing firmly. This sticks waxed or rubber cemented copy firmly to the layout sheet. If you are pasting up typewritten copy or press type, take special care not to smear the type.

Double check all alignments; make certain everything is straight.

Screened photos can be put into the final pasteup. But if you are using halftones, the printer will have to shoot them separately and strip them into the negative, so use transparent red *rubylith vinyl* where photos are to go. Ask for it at a graphic supply store, and cut it to fit the space the photo will occupy. This will create a clear area on the negative where the photo negatives can be stripped in later.

A large number of pasteup supplies are available and many different systems have been devised. Layout sheets are available with varying sizes of grids. Pick the one that fits your needs. Layout sheets are taped to the board with masking tape.

Sheets can be aligned with a T-square and triangle, or with a pre-punched alignment system; the latter is faster but costlier. Always leave the T-square resting against the same edge of the board. For ruling vertical lines, place the triangle against the T-square rather than moving the T-square. Do vertical alignment with the triangle, horizontal alignment with the T-square.

After copy is pasted in position, add any borders, lines or boxes, using special tape available in many widths and designs from art supply stores or catalogs. Remember to leave space for rules and borders when preparing a layout.

If a second color is to be used, its location is indicated with an overlay, usually a clear acetate sheet pasted up in the same manner as the other sheet. All copy of one color goes on one sheet. Sheets are stacked together to give the idea of overall appearance.

Once pasteup is completed, it's a good idea to do a photocopy of the whole thing to get a better idea of how it will look in print.

You'll probably run across typesetting errors in the last stages of pasteup. Single lines can be reset and pasted over the incorrect line. It's better to get the entire line reset than a single word, although single words can be inserted if the error doesn't change the spacing of the word.

## Copying and Printing

If you need only a small number of copies, you will probably copy the newsletter yourself, or if you do not have access to a good copying machine, have your "instant printer" do it.

If you want to use a printer, however, get bids. Make a list of specifications, including the number of copies, the dimensions of the pages, the number of pages, the paper stock and color, and the color or colors of ink you want. (More than one color will drive costs substantially higher.) If you want the printer to cut, collate, staple, and fold the newsletters, put those operations on the list. You can make up your own bid sheets, get them from a printer, or buy them from an art supply store. The important thing is to put specifications in writing.

Establish a clear understanding with your printer. A relationship of mutual trust and understanding will save time and trouble for you both. It's good to work with the same printer issue after issue. But when you contract with a printer for services, put a clause in permitting you to cancel if the printer consistently fails to deliver on time or to meet standards of quality. Be clear about a fixed cost for standard specifications (as noted on the bid sheet), but allow some flexibility for one-time changes and variations in copy.

Look at samples of the printer's work, and talk to some of his active customers. Don't make cost the sole deciding factor in choosing a printer. Expect to do your part in building a good working relationship. Don't put pressure on him by constantly missing your own deadlines. He may be able to bail you out sometimes; at other times he won't.

If you remain flexible in your approach, you'll find that the printer can show you ways to save time and money by altering specifications. Encourage the printer to suggest ways to hold down or trim costs. Sometimes a printer will have enough paper left over from a large job that can be used for your newsletter—and will cost less than custom-ordered paper. A slight variation in paper weight or texture will probably not visibly affect the appearance of your publication.

If several photos are to be run on the same page, hold down printing costs by running them all their original size, or by having the printer shoot them all together—reducing or enlarging them all the same percentage.

If black and white begins to bore you, use a light-colored paper—it's much less expensive than running the pages through the press a second time to get a second color of ink. Beware of papers so dark that they muddy photographs and make print hard to read.

When deciding on the number of copies to make or order, allow for standard circulation plus extras for file or future use. A special story in an issue may be reason to print additional extra copies for special distribution. Look at the content of each issue and try to anticipate any clamor from the public to get copies of it.

## Distribution

Small circulation employee newsletters are often distributed by hand to employees at work. This method of distribution creates interaction and dialogue among fellow workers and provides immediate feedback.

But it has drawbacks. The newsletter is read hastily at work, if at all. Employees who do read it thoroughly lose productive time on the job. There's less chance the newsletter will be taken home—there to be read by family and friends.

To gain advantages, some organizations mail newsletters to employees at home.

## Mailing Lists

Organizations that mail newsletters must keep good mailing lists. Keeping lists up-to-date can entail much time and effort.

Labels for reader lists of fewer than 500 names can be most economically and efficiently handled by using the office copier to make new sets of pressure-sensitive labels. This works especially well if the mailing list changes little and if the names do not have to be sorted by zip code.

For lists up to 2,000 names, those that change constantly, and those that must be sorted by zip code, the majority use equipment for making metal plates or farm the jobs out to firms that deal in such address lists.

For lists of more than 2,000, using computer labels can be cost-efficient. Organizations with their own computers often handle their own mailing lists. For those without computers, most larger cities have computer firms that handle mailing lists.

The big cost is the initial one. But after names have been entered into the computer, the costs of adding and deleting names and of generating labels for each issue are nominal.

## Mailing Rates

There are four ways to mail newsletters.

*First class.* This is the most expensive, especially if your newsletter weighs more than an ounce. But it gets priority handling, and if getting the newsletter to readers quickly is essential, it may be the best way.

*Second class.* This is the cheapest way to mail newsletters but there are numerous requirements for qualifying for a second class permit. The newsletter must be typeset and printed by offset. It must be published regularly and have a publication office that is open during regular business hours. It must have a list of paid subscribers and be devoted primarily to news, not advertising. It must contain an identification statement within its first five pages. The cost of the permit depends on the size of the circulation.

*Third class bulk rate.* To qualify for a third class bulk rate permit, the mailing must be at least 200 pieces. There is a yearly fee plus a one-time only fee for the permit holder.

Newsletters must be sorted by zip code, bundled and bagged according to specific rules.

If you use third class bulk rate, it's a good idea to include your own name and address on the mailing list. You'll get a pretty good idea of when the newsletter is received by subscribers, which may be several days after delivery to the post office.

*Single piece third class.* For mailing fewer than 200 pieces of identical mail, you pay a set rate for newsletters weighing less than two ounces. No permit is required.

When using second or third class, preprint your postal permit indicia on the mailing space of your newsletter. It saves the time of putting on stamps and the cost of using envelopes.

Postal regulations and costs change continually and often affect size and printing standards. Ask local postal authorities to notify you of any changes.

For all but very small circulations, preparing newsletters for bulk mailing can be time consuming. Most mailing operations can be done by machine—folding, stuffing, sealing, stamping and addressing.

Calculate the cost per copy of doing this job yourself, including the wages of persons on the staff who do it. Chances are, the job can be farmed out to a mailing service that uses machines for less than it's costing you now.

# Appendix 1
# Model Stylebook

# MODEL STYLEBOOK

## 1. General manuscript preparation

1.1 Type stories on one side of a page only, and double- or triple-space the lines, leaving margins of at least one and one-half inches on all sides.

1.2 Do not divide a sentence from the bottom of one page to the top of the next.

1.3 Number all pages on the upper right corner.

1.4 Check grammar, spelling, punctuation and figures for accuracy.

1.5 Complete a story in all respects before turning it in.

1.6 Include all photographs and art work. If they are unavoidably delayed, list them and describe their contents and intended use in the story.

1.7 Write *30* at the end of the last page of the story manuscript, to indicate that that is the end of the story.

1.8 Make a photocopy of the story.

## 2. Punctuation

### *The Period*

2.1 The period is used after a declarative or imperative sentence: *There are 50 states. Count the people.*

2.2 The period is used in abbreviations: *the U.S., the U.N.*

2.3 The period is sometimes used after a statement that includes an implicit question: *I don't know why he would do that.*

### *The Comma*

2.4 The comma separates words and figures to avoid confusion: *What the solution is, is a question. August 1, 1984. There are 18,758 fans at the Grackles' game tonight.*

2.5 The comma separates items in a series: *The woman was tall, dark, and handsomely dressed.* If the last two items in a series are single words, the comma is not used, because it is clearly not needed to clarify meaning: *Hooray for the red, white and blue!*

2.6 The comma is used before *and, but, or, for* and *nor* when those connectives introduce second independent clauses into a sentence: *The day's cool, hazy atmosphere made her tired, but he was as full of energy as ever.*

If they do not, the comma is omitted: *The city looked perfectly lovely and, at the same time, exuded a kind of dull energy.* Short main clauses may be separated by commas: *He ran, I rode my bike.*

2.7 The comma is used to set off nonrestrictive material: *His uncle, a good man, disliked cats. The work, he discovered, was exhausting.*

2.8 The comma should not separate a subject from its verb or a verb from its object.

## The Semicolon

2.9 The semicolon separates two medium-length or long independent clauses: *The gaudy drapes in the living room were offensive; they seemed to have been chosen by someone from outer space.* It is sometimes used to separate two such clauses introduced by connectives such as *and, or, but, for* and *nor* when the independent clauses they introduce are complex or have commas in them.

2.10 Semicolons are used for items in a series that have commas within them: *The party consisted of R. G. Austin; Sally Austin, his wife; Jane Austin, his mother; Anna Rabbit, her nurse; and Giles, the chauffeur.* (Without the semicolons, this could read as eight people; and, in fact, without the semicolon, it would be impossible to determine for sure who the various characters and roles in this line-up are.)

## The Apostrophe

2.11 The apostrophe indicates the possessive case of nouns: *Joel's skateboard, Crosby's obsession, the couple's dog, boys' wear, states' rights.*

2.12 The apostrophe is not used to indicate the possessive *its. The cat was playing with its yarn.* An apostrophe and *s* used with *it* means *it is. It's a great day for singing a song.*

2.13. Some unusual applications of apostrophe use: *for Jesus' sake, the Joneses' house, Moses' tablet.*

2.14 The apostrophe indicates the omission of figures: *class of '84, the fabulous '50s.*

2.15 When the apostrophe is not an official part of a name, don't use it: *Johns Hopkins University, Actors Equity Association.* Use it according to tradition: *the Court of St. James's.*

## The Colon

2.16 The colon introduces summary matter: lists, statements and conclusions that follow from preceding matter. It takes the place of an implied example: *After months of agonizing, he reached a decision: he couldn't make a decision. The $1,000,000 was left to his survivors: $999,000 to his dog, $1,000 to his son.*

2.17 The colon is used for academic and Biblical references: *Matthew 2:14. Gastroenterology 1980; 79:311-14.*

## The Exclamation Point

2.18 The exclamation point is used to indicate enthusiasm, surprise, incredulity or another strong emotion: *How wonderful! What! Come back here!* The exclamation point is fundamentally out of place in news writing.

## Parentheses

2.19 Parentheses set off closely related, nonrestrictive material from the text: *It is not the custom (at least in the areas he mentioned) to stand at attention during political speeches. "That idea," he said, "as explained by (Rep. Frank) Wright, is very appealing."*

2.20 When location identification is needed but is not part of an official group name, parentheses are used: *The Kansas City (MO) Historical Society.* They are not appropriately used to separate parts of essential information from each other: *The Kansas City, Kansas area population is 234,000.*

2.21 When the last part of a sentence is parenthetical, the punctuation goes outside the parentheses: *We will be living in Paris this fall (we hope, we hope). Nine persons out of ten live in the suburbs (see Figure 3).*

2.22 A complete sentence may be parenthesized, in which case, it takes its punctuation with it: *The Spruce Goose is the largest airplane ever built. (Its wing span is longer than 2 football fields!")*

## Quotation Marks

2.23 Quotation marks enclose direct statements by a person other than a writer: *He said, "Read it, it will change your life."* In quotes that are several paragraphs long, each paragraph begins with quote marks, but closing quote marks are used only once — at the end of the last paragraph.

2.24 Quotation marks are used on slang expressions, on words used as words in typewritten copy, and misnomers. They are sometimes used to show the writer's intent to be ironic: *She was "too busy" to visit her mother.*

2.25 In typewritten copy, use quotation marks on titles of books, plays, poems, movies, speeches, etc. In typeset copy, however, italicize such titles. Exceptions are speeches, short musical compositions, and titles of paintings and other works of art, which take quotation marks.

2.26 Use quotation marks on nicknames: *Jim "Moondog" Morey and Phil "Monsoon" McManus spent the evening listening to Richard "Little Richey" Lucente's Cajun band.*

2.27 Commas and periods are placed inside closing quotation marks; colons and semicolons are placed outside them. Other punctuation is placed according to meaning: *Why call it a "gentleman's agreement"? The question is, "Should we get married?" Doesn't her habit of saying "You know?" all the time bother you?*

2.28 Quotes within quotes are identified by double, then single marks, thus: *"The question is, 'Does his position violate the "gentlemen's 'post-haste' agreement" so eloquently described by my colleague as "tommyrot"?' "* (It would be better to rephrase a sentence than to write one like that.)

## The Dash

2.29 The dash indicates a sudden intrusion of a thought related to the subject. *He claimed—no one denied it—that he had priority. If that man should gain control—God forbid!—our troubles will have only begun.*

## The Hyphen

2.30 The hyphen forms compound words and expressions: *A-bomb, 20-20 vision, secretary-treasurer.*

2.31 The hyphen is used suspensively, to attach more than one adjective to a noun in such expressions as *low-to-moderate-income housing. . .14- and 15-year-olds.* (Note the space left before the *and.*)

2.32 When a prefix ends in and is followed by the same letter, a hyphen is sometimes used: *post-traumatic.* Check a current dictionary for hyphenation. Exceptions are many: *preempt, reelect, cooperate, coed, coordinate.* Prefixes such as *demi, semi, bi, tri, co, pre, re, sub, super, inter, intra, anti, over* and *under* are usually joined to a word without a hyphen.

2.33 The hyphen is not used with adverbs. Do not use it with words ending in *ly*: *badly damaged, fully informed, newly chosen.*

2.34 The hyphen may serve to distinguish meanings of identically spelled words: *recover, re-cover, resent, re-sent.*

2.35 The hyphen separates a prefix from a capitalized proper noun: *un-American, pre-Norman.*

2.36 The prefix *ex* is hyphenated: *ex-wife, ex-officio.*

2.37 Fractions are hyphenated: *one and one-half years ago, 10 one-and-one-half-year-olds.*

2.38 Do not hyphenate words formed with the suffixes *like* or *wide: childlike, citywide.*

2.39 Do not hyphenate such combinations as *vice president* and *surgeon general.*

2.40 Hyphenate nouns that express a double occupation: *writer-editor, architect-planner.*

## Italics

2.41 Use italics in typeset roman copy to identify words, phrases and letters meant to stand out from the rest of the text. In italic text, use roman type to make words stand out. Mind your *p's* and *q's*; *Mind your* p's *and* q's. I am reading *Ulysses*; *I am reading* Ulysses.

# 3. Capitalization

3.1 Capitalize a title preceding a name: *Board Chairman Shawn McArthur.* But do not capitalize such titles when they stand alone or follow a name: *Richard Davis, executive director.*

3.2 Capitalize official titles used before names: *Mayor Charles Wheeler, Governor Joseph Teasdale.* But write: *the mayor, the governor; Charles Wheeler, mayor of Kansas City; John Carlin, governor of Kansas; Charles Price, ambassador to Belgium,* or *the ambassador.*

3.3 Do not capitalize long titles that follow a name: *Alan Doan, first vice president in charge of marketing.*

3.4 Do not capitalize occupational titles such as *pianist Oscar Peterson, rookie left-handed pitcher Bill Lafferty, defense attorney Tom Loughlin.* (Do not separate such titles from names with a comma.)

3.5 Capitalize *U.S. Congress, Iowa Senate, Maine Legislature.* But write: *The state legislature passed the bill.* (Note: the building is the Capitol; the city is the capital.)

3.6 Capitalize *the States* when referring to the United States, but do not capitalize *national, federal* or *government* used as adjectives: *the national group, the legislative body.* Capitalize *State* used as part of an official title: *State Highway Department.* But write *the state, the region, the county* and *the city* in later references.

3.7 Capitalize the names of federal legislative bodies and committees: *Congress, Senate, House, U.S. Foreign Affairs Committee.* Do not capitalize adjective forms such as *congressinal, legislative* and *senatorial.* Write *the committee* in later references, once the full title has been established in a story.

3.8 Capitalize *Social Security Administration.* But write: *He was an advocate of social security provisions for retirees.*

3.9 Capitalize *U.S. Army, U.S. Navy, U.S. Marines,* but write: *the army, the navy, the marines* and *soldier, sailor, marine.*

3.10 Capitalize holiday names, historic events, observation weeks, hurricanes: *Labor Day, Battle of the Bulge, Easter, National Safety Week, Hurricane Gilda.*

3.11 Capitalize specific regions: *Middle East, Midwest, Arctic Circle, Upper Peninsula, the Orient, the East* (meaning the Orient). But do not capitalize words that merely indicate direction: *It is east of here, west of there, in the northern part of the state, on the east coast.*

3.12 Capitalize names of political parties, social and fraternal organizations: *Republican, Kappa Kappa Gamma, Knights of Columbus.*

3.13 Capitalize names of people and races: *Caucasian, Asian, Chinese, Negro, Native American, Cajun.* Use lower case, however, for *black people* and *white people, blacks* and *whites.*

3.14 Capitalize a common noun used in a formal name: *Hoover Dam, Missouri River, Cassidy County Courthouse, Wall Street.* But write *the dam, the river, the courthouse* and *the street* in later references.

3.15 Capitalize trade names and use trade or registration marks with them on first reference: *Xerox®, Q-tips®.*

3.16 Capitalize titles of books, plays, poems, paintings, etc.: *Paris Was Yesterday, A Chorus Line, The Road Not Taken,* "*The Girl in White*" (painting).

3.17 Capitalize the first word of a quote introduced by a comma or a colon only if the quote is a complete sentence. *Franklin said, "A penny saved is a penny earned." Did Hamlet say, "O that this too, too sullied flesh would melt. . ."? He said the plan was "ridiculous beyond belief."*

3.18 Capitalize Biblical references and fanciful appellations and award names: *the Bible, a Biblical character, Buckeye State, Show-me State, Operation Breakthrough, Medal of Honor, Nobel Peace Prize.*

3.19 Do not capitalize *plan, report, project* or *study* unless the word is part of an official title.

## 4. Spelling

The neutral, central vowel sound of most unstressed syllables in English is the *schwa* (symbol ə). If it can be said to be pronounced at all, it is pronounced as a very weak *uh* sound: *ago,* agent, maintenance, incredible, bachelor. The only guide to spelling words containing schwas is to memorize them. Try a mnemonic (memory-aiding) device such as magnifying in your mind the syllable containing the schwa: *baLANCE, indepenDENT, eliGIBLE, sponSOR, foREIGN.*

4.1 Words like *niece, receive* and *friend* are frequently misspelled. The order of the vowels in the *ie* combination is generally stated in the jingle: "Write *i* before *e* except after *c* or when sounded as *ay* as in *neighbor* and *weigh*".

Some other common words spelled with *ei* are *counterfeit*, *either*, *foreign*, *forfeit*, *height*, *heir*, *leisure*, *neither*, *seize* and *sovereign*.

4.2 *Homonyms* sound alike but have different meanings and, usually, different spellings: *altar* and *alter*, *peace* and *piece*, *weak* and *week*. A writer working fast and thinking phonetically may use the spelling of one when he or she intends the other.

Here are some pairs of homonyms that give frequent trouble: *affect (to produce an effect upon)* and *effect (to make*, or as a noun, roughly, *result)*; *all together (all at once)* and *altogether (wholly* or *thoroughly)*; *canvas (cloth)* and *canvass (to solicit)*; *council (group)* and *counsel (to advise* or, as a noun, *lawyer)*; *forward (ahead)* and *foreword (preface)*; *its (belonging to it)* and *it's (it is)*; *precede (to go or come before)* and *proceed (to move along a course)*; *who's (who is)* and *whose (belonging to whom)*.

4.3 Since most English nouns take *s* plurals, all plurals formed in any other way are considered irregular. The troublesome plurals are those ending in *o* or *y*. Such nouns have regular *s* plurals when the *o* or *y* immediately follows a vowel: *cameos, keys, attorneys, donkeys, valleys, folios, radios, studios*. They are generally irregular when the *o* or *y* follows a consonant: *buffaloes, cargoes, echoes, heroes, potatoes, torpedoes, vetoes*.

The chief exceptions are musical terms: *altos, bassos, oratorios, pianos, solos, sopranos*. Others are *autos, cantos, dynamos, Eskimos, halos, mementos, provisos* and *quartos*.

Plurals of nouns ending in a consonant plus *y* are formed by changing the *y* to *i* before adding *es*: *allies, babies, cities, cries, tries*.

4.4 Plurals of nouns ending in *s, ss, sh, ch, x* or *z* are formed by simply adding *es*: Jameses, ashes, bunches, taxes, foxes, buzzes. Some exceptions: *bass, fish, perch, six's, ellipses, theses.*

4.5  In words of one syllable, the final consonant is usually doubled before a suffix beginning with a vowel if the word ends in a single consonant and contains a single vowel: *war, warring, tap, tapped.*

This rule extends to words of more than one syllable *if* the accent falls on the last syllable: *preFER, preferred; BENefit, benefited; conFER, conferring.*

4.6  When a suffix beginning with a consonant is added to a word ending in a silent *e*, the *e* is retained: *achievement, extremely, indefinitely, sincerely.* Exceptions: *argument, awful, duly, ninth, probably, wholly.*

*Abridgment, acknowledgment* and *judgment* are preferred to the also acceptable spellings *abridgement, acknowledgement* and *judgement.*

4.7  When a suffix beginning with a vowel is added to a word ending in silent *e*, the *e* is dropped unless it is required to indicate pronunciation or to avoid confusion with a similar word: *accumulating, achieving, boring, coming, grievance, icy.* Exceptions are: (to keep a *c* or *g* soft): *advantageous, changeable, courageous, manageable, noticeable, outrageous, peaceable, serviceable, singeing, tingeing, vengeance;* (to prevent mispronunciation), *canoeist, eyeing, hoeing, mileage, shoeing;* (to prevent confusion with other words) *dyeing.*

4.8  Words ending with the sound *seed* are usually spelled *cede: accede, concede, intercede, precede, recede, secede.* There are four exceptions: *exceed, proceed, succeed* and *supersede.*

4.9  Here are some often used and frequently misspelled words:

| | | | | |
|---|---|---|---|---|
| accommodate | exhilarate | irrelevant | paralleled | siege |
| acknowledgment | existence | judgment | Philippines | skillful |
| adviser | fulfill | liaison | Portuguese | stabilize |
| all right | guerrilla | lightning | privilege | tranquility |
| bouillon | gypsy | liquefy | resistance | vilify |
| canister | harass | marshal | restaurateur | weird |
| diarrhea | hemorrhage | minuscule | salable | |
| ecstasy | inoculate | nickel | scurrilous | |
| embarrass | iridescent | niece | sergeant | |

4.10 Most prefixes and suffixes are written *solid*, i.e., without the hyphen. Exceptions are noted. Some general rules for prefixes and suffixes:

all (hyphenated): all-star
ante, anti: *antebellum*, *antiestablishment* (except in proper noun usage such as *anti-American*)
bi: *biennial*, *bifocal*
co: *copilot*, *coed* but *co-worker*
counter: *counterfoil*, *counteract*
down: *downstroke*, *touchdown*
electro: *electrolysis*, *electrolyte*
ex (hyphenated): *ex-champion*
extra: *extraterrestrial*, *extramarital*
fold: *twofold*
in (prefix): *insufferable*; (suffix hyphenated): *stand-in*
infra: *infrared*
inter: *interstate*, *intergalactic*
intra: *intrastate*, *intramural*
multi: *multimillion*, *multifaceted*
non: *nonpartisan*, *nonsupport*
out: (hyphenated): *out-talk*, *out-box*
over: *overcome*, *pushover*
post: *postwar*, *postpartum*
pre: *predetermine*, *prewar*
self (hyphenated): *self-defense*, *self-respect*
semi: *semiannual*
sub: *subfreezing*
super: *superabundant*
trans: *transatlantic*, *transcontinental* (but trans-American)
tri: *trifocal*
ultra: *ultraviolet*
un: *unshaven*, *unnecessary* (but un-American)
under: *underground*, *undersold*
wide: *areawide*, *worldwide*

## 5. Abbreviations

5.1 In first mention, names of organizations should be spelled out (*American Medical Association, Centers for Disease Control*), and the abbreviation should follow the name in parentheses. Thereafter in the story, the abbreviation may be used:

> The Kansas City Metropolitan Region (KCMR) includes two more counties than the city's Standard Metropolitan Statistical Area (SMSA).
>
> The report was submitted to the Department of Housing and Urban Development (HUD).

Note: Periods are not used in most such abbreviations.

5.2 Abbreviate St., Ave., Blvd., Ter., in addresses, but not Point, Port, Circle, Plaza, Place, Drive, Oval, Road, Lane: *16 E. 72d St.; 16 Gregory Ave. NW* (no periods in NW); *Sunset Boulevard, Main Street, Fifth Avenue* (where no specific address is given).

Highways are written as numbers: *I-35, US 69, US 71 Bypass, M-7, K-10.*

5.3 Lower case abbreviations usually take periods. The rule is that if the letters form words, periods are needed: *c.o.d., f.o.b.*

5.4 Abbreviate state names when they follow the name of a city. Omit the name of the state after a city if the city is sufficiently well known without it.

Traditionally, abbreviations for the states are: *Ala., Ariz., Ark., Calif., Colo., Conn., Del., Fla., Ga., Il., Ind., Ks., Ky., La., Md., Mass., Mich., Minn., Miss., Mo., Mont., Neb., Nev., N.C., N.D., N.H., N.J., N.M., N.Y., Okla., Ore., Pa., R.I., S.C., S.D., Tenn., Tex., Vt., Va., Wash., Wis., W.Va.* and *Wyo.*; and *Alaska, Hawaii, Idaho, Iowa, Ohio, Maine* and *Utah* are not abbreviated.

In addresses, use the official U.S. Postal Service two-letter state abbreviations, designated in capitals: *AL, AK, AZ, AR,*

CA, CO, CT, *DE, DC,* FL, GA, KS, KY, LA, ME, MD, MA, MI, MN, MS, MO, MT, NB, NV, NH, NJ, NM, NY, NC, ND, OH, OK, OR, PA, RI, SC, SD, TN, TX, UT, VT, VA, WA, WV, WI, WY.

5.5 Abbreviate *United Nations* and *United States* in titles: *U.S. Chamber of Commerce.* Otherwise spell them out.

5.6 Abbreviate and capitalize religious, fraternal, scholastic or honorary degrees, but use lower case when they are spelled out: *B.S., bachelor of science.*

5.7 Abbreviate and capitalize titles such as: *Mr., Mrs., Ms., Mlle., Dr., Prof., Sen., Rep., Asst., Lt. Gov., Gen., Supt., Atty. Gen.* before names but not after. *President* is not abbreviated in any use.

5.8 Do not abbreviate months in sentences; write *October 12, 1942.* Abbreviations used in tabular matter are: *Jan., Feb., Mar., Apr., Jun., Jul., Aug., Sept., Oct., Nov., Dec. May* requires no abbreviation.

5.9 Days of the week are abbreviated only in tabular matter, where they are: *Mon., Tue., Wed., Thu., Fri., Sat.,* and *Sun.* On calendars, M, T, W, T, F, S and S is acceptable use.

5.10 Abbreviate *St.* in *St. Louis, St. Paul, St. Petersburg.* Abbreviate the mountain but spell the city: *Mt. Everest, Mount Vernon.* Abbreviate the army post name but spell the city: *Ft. Leavenworth, Fort Meyer.*

5.11 Spell out percent (one word) and use figures before it: *8 percent.*

5.12 Names of foreign countries are not abbreviated.

# 6. Numbers

6.1 In general text, spell out *one* through *nine* and use numerals for *10* and over: *one time, three days, 18 children, 50 years, 78 women, 200 delegates.*

6.2 Use numerals to state specific or technical measurements, dates, times of day and page numbers: *4x6 feet,*

*8½x11-inch paper, 4 cubic feet, 92 degrees, 15 percent, 2,289 votes, 35mm film, 45-rpm record; July 14, 1983 or 14 July 1983; 6 p.m., 5:30 a.m.; page 5, pages 11-17.*

For casual statements of measure, i.e., of height, weight, length and volume, however, follow the general rule of writing out numbers under 10:*the room looked about eight feet wide; the page had one-inch margins; the pool was nine and one-half feet deep; a four-pound roast; five feet tall; six pints.*

6.3 When one numeral follows another, avoid confusion by alternating styles of usage or rewriting the sentence: *eleven 45-rpm records; one hundred 20-cent stamps (or 100 twenty-cent stamps); ten 4-foot boards, 200 fives.* Do not let one number stand next to another if there is any chance of confusion. Recast the sentence to avoid such a construction as: *Of the 324, 168 already have been obtained.*

6.4 When a number begins a sentence it must be spelled out. If the number is very long, rewrite the sentence to avoid opening with it.

6.5 Poetic and idiomatic numbers are spelled: *A thousand times no! I've told you a hundred times.*

6.6 Write out *million, billion* and *trillion: $1 million, $300 billion, $10 trillion, a million times.*

An exact amount can be written: *$4,251,756.*

The decimal is carried to two places: *$4.25 million.*

6.7 Ordinary sums of money follow the general rule: *nine dollars; 25 cents; a two-dollar hat; $10; a $250 donation; $650,000.*

6.8 When combinations of large and small numbers are used in one passage to refer to like subjects, use the rule for the larger numbers: *The group was made up of 7 children, 43 women, and 32 men; He paid $8 for his Hackysack; I paid $11 for mine.*

6.9 Use numerals for statistical material, tables and charts, and in numbers with decimals.

6.10 Use numerals for military units, political divisions, and court districts. Write: *6th Fleet, 10th ward.*

# 7. Grammar

Building a sentence is like building anything else. There are certain basic parts to work with. In English these parts are subjects, verbs, complements, modifiers and connectives. They occur in units called phrases and clauses. Clauses have subjects and verbs. Phrases do not.

The number of clauses in a sentence and the relationship(s) between or among them determine basic sentence structure.

## *The Simple Sentence*

7.1  The basic English sentence is one independent clause (it stands alone) made up of a subject, a verb and a complement. (The last is usually an object or a predicate adjective.)

A sentence so structured is called a simple sentence:

*Joe hit John.* (*John* is the direct object.)

*I am cold.* (*Cold* is a predicate adjective.)

When an intransitive verb is used, the simple sentence basic structure is only a subject and verb:

*George laughed.*

*We have been fooled.*

The simple sentence may have more than one subject:

*Joe and George laughed.*

It may have more than one verb:

*Joe sang and danced.*

It may have more than one of both:

*Joe, John and George sang, laughed and danced.*

It may take more than one complement:

*Joe gave me this book.* (Complements are *book*, a direct object, and *me*, an indirect object.)

*George laughed at John and Joe.*

A simple sentence may consist of only one word—a verb, with the subject understood:

*Leave.* (Subject *you* understood.)

*See?* (Subject *you* and auxiliary verb *do* understood.)

*It* can carry a lot of baggage in modifiers:

*Early in the morning on a dismal, rainy day, silly old David reluctantly gave ungrateful me this incredibly ratty, beat-up, dirty, old book.*

No matter how many modifying phrases you hang on a simple sentence, its basic structure does not change. The structure changes when you add another clause. When you do, you have a complex sentence or a compound sentence.

## The Complex Sentence

7.2  A complex sentence contains one independent clause and one or more dependent clauses. (Dependent clauses do not stand alone; they need an independent clause to lean on.)

*After our work was done,* we all ran to the bar. (Introductory adverb clauses that tell where, when, how or why take commas.)

*Smile when you say that.*

*That he was a fool was obvious.* (Introductory noun clauses do not take commas.)

*This is the day that the Lord hath made.* (Restrictive adjective clauses do not take commas.)

My uncle, *who travels constantly,* will be here tonight. (Nonrestrictive adjective clauses take commas. If you have more than one uncle, but only one who travels constantly, the phrase becomes *restrictive,* i.e., a piece of essential information, and the commas are omitted.)

These words usually mark the onset of a dependent clause: *after, although, as (as if), before, because, how, if, since, than, that, though, unless, until, what, when, where, whereas, whether, while, why, which, who, whom, whose.*

Can you tell which of these is a simple sentence, which is a complex one?

1. *Early in the morning Sam and I headed down the river, fished for a while, and then just lay back watching the clouds all day.*

2. *When we came home, it was dark.*

If you use a dependent clause alone, you have committed an error—the fragment.

*That you are all happy with your work.*

*When we got home tired and hungry from our long walk.*

1. Simple        2. Complex

## The Compound Sentence

7.3 The third basic sentence type is the compound sentence, which contains two or more independent clauses joined by the connectives *and, but, nor* or *for* used with a comma:

*Joe had been hitting John for two hours, but John continued to turn away.*

*You have to humor Joe, or he'll write an awful story about you.*

*George won't hit John, nor will he hit Joe.*

Two independent clauses joined with a semicolon also make a compound sentence:

*Joe begged her to dance; reluctantly, Jane refused.*

If you join two independent clauses with a comma and no connective you have committed an error—the comma splice:

*We were in the theater watching the movie for two hours, he was home all the time.*

But two very short independent clauses may be joined with a comma:

*He sang, I danced.*

*You were cold, I was hungry.*

## The Compound-Complex Sentence

7.4 The fourth sentence type is the compound-complex sentence, which contains two or more independent clauses and one or more dependent clauses:

*We watched for a long time, but I could not see if he was watching us; she said he was.*

*He pushed and I pulled until we were exhausted.*

## Common Errors in Sentence Structure

*7.5 Fragments.* A fragment is an incomplete construction. It usually results from mistaking a subordinate clause for a main clause, a verbal for a verb:

*The Tigers made two runs in the ninth. Thus tying the score.* (Fragment.)

*The Tigers made two runs in the ninth, thus tying the score.* (Correct.)

*The Tigers made two runs in the ninth. Which was when they tied the score.* (Fragment.)

*When the Tigers made two runs in the ninth, they tied the score.* (Correct.)

*It was difficult to decide which choice to make. To return to work, or to go swimming.* (Fragment.)

*It was difficult to decide whether to return to work or go swimming.* (Correct.)

*It was a wonderful week. Fishing and swimming every day and dancing every night.* (Fragment.)

*It was a wonderful week. We fished and swam every day and danced every night.* (Correct.)

*7.6 Fused sentences.* Failure to separate two independent clauses by connective or punctuation results in a fused sentence:

*I knocked on the door when the lady came I gave her my most ingratiating smile.* (Fused.)

*I knocked on the door. When the lady came, I gave her my most ingratiating smile.* (Correct.)

*It is difficult to believe he said that what could he have been thinking.* (Fused.)

*It is difficult to believe he said that. What could he have been thinking?* (Correct.)

*7.7 Comma splice.* The joining of two main clauses with a comma instead of a period or semicolon is called a comma splice:

*His chances of election are not good because the independent voters do not like him, it would be safer to nominate another candidate.* (Comma splice.)

*His chances of election are not good because the independent voters do not like him. It would be safer to nominate another candidate.* (Correct.)

*This is the best book I have ever read, it kept me up all night.* (Comma splice.)

*This is the best book I have ever read; it kept me up all night.* (Correct.)

Sometimes a comma splice can be corrected by the addition of a coordinating connective. This method specifies the relationship between the two main clauses:

*She says that she does not like football, I doubt that she has seen two games in her life.* (Comma splice.)

*She says that she does not like football, but I doubt that she has seen two games in her life.* (Correct.)

*It will cost a great deal of money, there is no guarantee that the plan will succeed.* (Comma splice.)

*It will cost a great deal of money, and there is no guarantee that the plan will succeed.* (Correct.)

Sometimes it is reasonable to subordinate one clause to another in order to correct a comma splice, and, again, to specify the relationship between the clauses:

*He is discouraged about flunking, I think he will drop the class.* (Comma splice.)

*He is so discouraged about flunking that I think he will drop the class.* (Correct.)

Two main clauses joined by a transitional connective (*consequently, however, moreover, nevertheless, therefore*) take a semicolon or a period between them:

*I admit that he is honest and conscientious, nevertheless, I will not vote for him.* (Comma splice.)

*I admit that he is honest and conscientious; nevertheless I will not vote for him.* (Correct.)

Two short main clauses that are closely related may be joined by a comma:

*I passed, he doubled.*

*The women like him, the men don't.*

*7.8 Faulty parallelism.* The convention of parallelism is that elements serving the same purpose in a sentence should have the same grammatical structure.

Thus, two or more sentence elements arranged in a series or joined by a coordinating connective should have the same form: a phrase should be followed by a phrase, a clause by a clause, a noun by a noun, and a verb by a verb.

*The commission has the power of investigation, conciliation, holding hearings, subpoena witnesses, issue cease and desist commands, order reinstatement of a discharged employee, and direct the hiring of a qualified applicant.* (Faulty parallelism.)

*The commission has the power to investigate, to conciliate, to hold hearings, to subpoena witnesses, to issue cease and desist commands, to order reinstatement of a discharged employee, and to direct the hiring of a qualified applicant.* (Correct parallelism.)

*7.9 Dangling modifiers.* A dangling modifier is one that has nothing in the sentence to modify:

*By going to the various meetings and cocktail parties on the political circuit, my conversation, manners and poise became more polished.* (Dangling modifier. His conversation, manners and poise did not go to parties.)

*By going to the various meetings and cocktail parties on the political circuit, I was able to polish my conversation, manners and poise.* (Phrase modifies *I*, the missing subject in the faulty construction above.)

*In order to be served, shirts and shoes must be worn.* (Dangling modifier; shirts and shoes are not served, people are.)

*In order to be served, customers must wear shirts and shoes.* (Correct.)

(Or the admirably direct:) *No shirt, no shoes, no service.* The implied full thought is grammatically correct: If you wear no shirt and no shoes, you will get no service.

*Walking downtown, a streetcar jumped the tracks.* (Faulty.)

*Walking downtown, I saw a streetcar jump the tracks.* (Correct.)

*When only five years old, my mother died.* (Faulty.)

*When I was only five years old, my mother died.* (Correct.)

*Although working full time on an outside job, my grades remained good.* (Faulty.)

*Although I was working full time on an outside job, my grades remained good.* (Correct.)

*7.10 Shifts in subjects and verbs.* Awkward shifts in structure usually take one of two forms: shifts of subject within a sentence or paragraph, and shifts of verb tense.

*When you get through with an ordeal like that, a person is exhausted.* (Awkward shift.)

*When you get through with an ordeal like that, you are exhausted.* (Correct.)

*I did not like to refuse his invitation, but you can't spend all your time going to shows.* (Awkward shift.)

*I did not like to refuse his invitation, but I can't spend all my time going to shows.* (Correct.)

*As the centuries passed, the dress patterns become more and more complicated.* (Awkward shift.)

*As the centuries passed, the dress patterns became more and more complicated.* (Correct.)

*7.11 Incomplete constructions.* The omission of words necessary for a clear understanding of the thought often results in an ambiguous sentence.

*Statistics show that college men like their studies better than women.* (Incomplete construction.)

*Statistics show that college men like their studies better than women do.* (Correct.)

*Today is as hot, if not hotter than any day this summer.* (Incomplete construction.)

*Today is as hot as, if not hotter than, any other day we've had this summer.* (Correct.)

# Appendix 2
## Model
# Headline Schedule

## MODEL HEADLINE SCHEDULE

This model is given only as an example, not as a general direc-
tive. The four categories listed are not mutually exclusive; e.g., a
headline for a main news story may sometimes be taken from the
styles for secondary stories. A feature headline may be any of the
sizes or styles given, depending on the weight and length of the
feature story. The model styles are given as a rule to follow; rules
have exceptions. Writing and counting headlines can be so complex and so trying that the writer will choose whatever style and
size will fit a story and announce it in the right words. The
general principle to remember, however, is that headline size and
style express story importance and character.

The assumed format of the model schedule newsletter page is
8½x11 inches. Two typefaces are used: Goudy Old Style, a serif
face, and Helvetica, a sans serif face. Within these families, seven
fonts are used:

# Goudy 30-pt bold

## Goudy 24-pt bold

## *Goudy 24-pt bold italic*

*Goudy 14-pt bold italic*

# *Helvetica 24-pt med ital*

## *Helvetica 18-pt medium italic*

Helvetica 12-pt medium

The traditional headline-writing practice of capitalizing all words except articles and prepositions is used. (More modern usage in newspapers is to write headlines with the capitalization rules that apply to sentences.)

1. Headlines for main stories are run 30-point Goudy bold roman and 24-point Goudy bold roman or italic. They are run across the page on one line, with or without a small *kicker* line above in 14-point bold italic. (The kicker should not run more than halfway across the main head.)

# Time's Short for Action on Medicare

(30 pt G bold rom)

# Board Recommends Solar Heating Project

(24 pt G bold rom)

*Appeals Also Made to Washington* (14 pt G bold ital kicker)

# *Suit Filed as Decision Nears on Air Base*

(24 pt G bold ital)

2. Headlines for secondary stories in two- and three-column formats are run in 18- or 24-point Helvetica medium italic, across one, two or three columns, with or without a *deck*, i.e., a two-line subhead in 14-point Goudy bold italic.

# Minority Firm Awarded Nutrition Contract Again

(24 pt H med ital, 2-column head on 3-column page)

# Bike Rules Changed Again

(18 pt H med ital, 1-column head on 2-column page)

# New Law Offers Incentives To Save Historic Buildings

## Funding Prospects Bright For Watkins Historic Site

(18 pt H med ital, 1-column head on 2-column page;
14 pt G bold ital deck, centered under main head)

3. Headlines for feature stories may be any of the styles in classes 1, 2 and 4. The size and style of the feature head should indicate its importance in relation to the other stories in a given issue. Features are often set off by boxes or rules or other graphic amenities such as screens.

### President's Message

# Gift to Minors Act Averts Heavy Taxes

(24 pt G bold roman; 1 column head on 2-column page; 12 pt H med roman *kicker*)

4. Headlines for short items and news stories, i.e., those only one to three paragraphs long usually run across one column. Any type size and style in the schedule may be used, depending on how much importance is attached to the story. Examples given are all 18-point Helvetica medium italic, one-column heads for a three-column format. These heads, as shown, may be written on one, two or three lines.

*Keyes Elected*

*Keyes Elected*
*Vice President*

*Keyes Elected*
*Vice President*
*Of State Group*

# Appendix 3
# Formula Stories

## FORMULA STORIES

Fresh writing marks good news stories. Imaginative reporters look for a way to write each story, one that captures what is unique in that story.

Readers tire of seeing the same kind of stories written the same way time after time. Yet, the formula story has its place. Some stories just don't have enough to them to lend themselves to anything but routine treatment. They are not worth the time it would take to find an unusual way to write them. They will be read because of who or what is involved even if the news is not of great importance.

Stories of routine promotions and transfers of employees, and stories about new policies are examples of this kind of story.

There is another reason for handling certain stories in a category the same way—it's democratic. It would be unfair, for example, to write a long detailed story about one employee's promotion, and a short, bare bones story about the similar promotion of another employee. That's why newspapers often handle obituaries and wedding stories in a standard form, with only rare exceptions for truly prominent or unusual people.

Beginning news writers learn by imitation. When they are assigned a story, they look for similar stories in the news. This not only gets them on the right track, but serves as a checklist to remind them of what should be included in the story. As they become more experienced and more confident they seek new ways to write a story, ways to make it more inviting to the reader.

The following examples will serve as a guide for writing certain basic kinds of stories.

### Personnel Items

The routine personnel item, such as a promotion or a transfer, should get right to the point:

*Susan Lawrence has been promoted to Associate Director. Lawrence, who joined the Arts Council three years ago as an executive assistant, was instrumental in the establishment of the Historic Preservation Council.*

*She received her bachelor's degree in art and architecture criticism from Harvard University in 1979 and is now studying for a master's degree in business at Rockhurst College.*

In writing these stories, avoid such effusive expressions as: "Congratulations are in order to. . ." and "Hard work has paid off for. . ." Stick to the facts. Who got promoted to what? How long has she been with the organization? What did she do previously? What did she study at school?

There is a natural curiosity about new employees. In general news stories, however, avoid rambling on about matters that have no bearing on the story. New employee stories may legitimately report that the employee is married and has three children or fought in Vietnam.

## Meetings

Many newsletter stories originate at meetings. It is not sufficient to start such a story by saying a meeting was held, that such-and-such was discussed and so-and-so attended it.

Find out what happened at the meeting. What was accomplished? What was said? Start with the most important result of the meeting:

*Members of the Audobon Society are urged to form car pools as part of an effort to conserve gasoline. A resolution adopted at the national board meeting last week called for all member chapters to join the effort to combat the national shortage of gasoline.*

*Jenkin David, board chairman, said that our efforts will. . .*

The story would go on to list details of how car pools would be set up and operated. It would itemize other action taken by the board, and it would give specific quotes and actions by individual society members or chapters.

If a meeting produces several results of nearly equal importance, the customary way to open the story is to summarize the action:

> *Funding for a $4 million interchange at I-72 and Robb Road, a $2 million improvement to the Green River sewage system, and a new $740,000 sanitary landfill was approved by the Roanoke Planning Commission last week.*
>
> *The interchange will connect highways 72 and. . .*

The story would go on to give details of each project, the background, what commission members had to say about the proposals, pro and con, and what the final vote was.

When a meeting produces no results, the reporter is sometimes hard pressed to find a news angle. Usually, there's something to be written:

> *After four hours of debate, the Spellman Community Hospital board voted to delay action on whether to seek federal funds for five new emergency medical vehicles until it could determine whether the hospital or the county would have responsibility for administering the expanded program. . .*

## Speeches

Reporting speeches follows the same pattern as reporting meetings. Single out the most important point the speaker made, document it in the paragraphs following the lead, then list other points made by the speaker:

> *There is no better way to prove the need for a regional*

*council than to look at the metropolitan area from the air, according to Walt Bodine.*

*Bodine, local broadcast-journalist and author, was principal speaker to more than 500 persons at the annual dinner meeting of the Mid-America Regional Council in late January.*

*"Go up in an airplane and fly over this great, sprawling community of ours," Bodine said. "Strain your eyes, but you won't see any state or county lines down below. From that lofty perspective, city limit signs are not very real."*

*Neighboring communities must work together to solve their problems, Bodine said. Those problems include. . .*

If several points are to be stressed they can be combined in the lead, then documented in separate paragraphs following the lead:

*New buses, expanded routes, more frequent service, and round-the-clock scheduling will all be needed to provide good mass transportation service to citizens of Dallas, Richard Davis, chairman of the Dallas Transit Authority, told regional transit officials last week.*

*In a speech, Davis called for. . .*

*First paragraph: (36 new buses)*

*Second paragraph: (41 more route miles of service)*

*Third paragraph: (14 maintenance and repair staff for a third shift)*

## Reports

Stories based on reports often start with the most important news and then itemize other elements of the report:

*The 1984 Farmland Industries general budget will be only 3 percent higher than the 1983 budget.*

*The increase was kept reasonable by the skillful handling of. . ."*

Sometimes there are so many elements in a report that the lead will focus on the report itself, then go on to list the elements:

*In a 105-page document, based on 2,500 pages of study, the Air Force has pictured the Kansas City area as it would be after nearly 4,000 military and civilian workers and their families leave Richards-Gebaur Air Force Base.*

*A draft Environmental Impact Statement compiled by the Air Force described the metropolis after the loss of population:*

*1. The housing market is loose and money is tight.*

*2. Tax revenues drop and unemployment rises.*

*3. The quality of neighborhoods wanes, rates of vandalism and fires climb.*

If a report is deadly dull, chances are that quotes taken from the report will be dull, too. A good way to enliven a report story is to interview the person or persons who prepared it, seeking candid, straightforward quotes to brighten the copy.

## Notices

A large number of stories are based on notices. They tell the reader that a specific action or event is scheduled at a certain hour, date and place. These stories take two basic forms:

*The deadline for filing applications for Section 8 housing funds is midnight June 30, the Department of Housing and Urban Development has announced.*

That's the direct approach. But often the reporter may want to interpret the importance of the event:

> *Students and faculty will have a chance to make their views known on the university's new merit pay policy at a hearing scheduled for next month.*
>
> *The hearing will be held at Allen Hall, 2406 Olentangy Road on December 11 at 7:30 p.m.*
>
> *Questionnaires will be circulated at the hearing. Participants will express their views in writing about whether the university should proceed with its plan to include student evaluation of faculty in the new policy.*
>
> *A transcript of the hearing and a tabulation of the questionnaires will be made public before the plan goes to the state legislature for final action.*

It is essential in notice stories to give the exact time, date and place an event is to be held.

But after the meeting has been held, this information is of little consequence. Too many newsletter stories about events that have already been held contain leads cluttered with this information:

> *On July 10, at 9 a.m., 400 employees of Hilton International gathered at Sailor Park for the annual picnic.*

Start the story with some news from the picnic—the softball teams' scores or outstanding plays. Or treat such a story as a feature. But the date should be generalized (*late last month, recently,* etc.) and, often with the location, placed farther down in the story.

## Controversies

Many good stories involve controversy. There's nothing wrong with starting such a story with the word itself:

> *A controversy over how to finance a proposed 911 emergency telephone system for the region has developed between*

*Bell Telephone Company and Yellow River Regional Council.*

Following the lead, give both sides of the controversy:

*Fletcher White, vice president of the phone company, criticized the council's recent proposal to add a surcharge to customers' bills to pay for the system. He said it should be financed by some form of tax.*

*Richard Nesbitt, executive director of the council, said a tax was not feasible because so many different cities would be involved. Furthermore, he said, the cities are located in two different states, each with different enabling statutes for taxation.*

These are a few suggested approaches for writing certain kinds of stories often encountered.

There are many others, of course, and there is nothing wrong with a beginning reporter reading local newspapers and other newsletters for ideas of how to write stories.

But the eventual goal is to break away from formula writing and seek novel ways to tell some stories.

# Appendix 4
# Form Contract

## FORM CONTRACT

This contract made this _____ day of _____, 198____, between _____, the company, having an office at _____ and _____, the contractor, having an office at_____.

### WITNESSETH:

That in consideration of the agreements expressed herein, the Company and the Contractor do hereby agree as follows:

ONE: The Contractor agrees to perform the following, hereinafter referred to as the "work":

Set in type, print, and perform related activities necessary to provide _____ copies per issue of the monthly publication, (name) as set forth in Attachments A & B.

All work shall be done in a good and workmanlike manner and to the satisfaction of the Company's representative.

TWO: The work to be performed shall be commenced and completed as follows:

Contract shall become effective on _____ and terminate on _____. Company shall have the option to renew this contract for two successive one-year terms upon the same conditions as herein provided except as to "contract price" which shall be mutually agreed upon at time of renewal. Company shall exercise said option by notifying Contractor in writing at least 30 days prior to expiration of the initial term, or renewal term, as the case may be.

THREE: Company shall pay to Contractor and Contractor agrees to accept in full payment for the work the following (state monthly amount), hereinafter called the "contract price." The sum to be paid to Contractor for the work includes any and all local, state and federal taxes, charges, and excises that may be imposed upon Contractor in connection with performance of this Contract. Contractor expressly assumes and agrees to pay the same. Final payment shall not be due and owing until (thirty) days have elapsed after completion of the work and after compliance with the conditions of Provision Five.

FOUR: Company's representative is _____ person designated by Company.

FIVE: Final payment shall be due and owing by Company after completion of all work, acceptance of work by Company, after receipt of the final bill and after the elapse of time stated in Provision Three. But Company may require Contractor to give evidence that all claims arising under the Contract have been satisfied and Contractor will reimburse Company for any money the latter may be compelled to pay for labor, material and other obligations.

SIX: Contractor shall be responsible for any material delivered to it by Company and return all material not required for completion of the work.

SEVEN: Contractor shall maintain complete and accurate records of labor, material and equipment. Company may inspect said records at all reasonable times.

EIGHT: The Company may reject any or all of the work if, in its opinion, same is not in accordance with this Contract. The Contractor shall repair or replace any rejected work within 24 hours after receiving written notice from the Company if notice is given during progress of the work. If notice is given following completion of the work, Contractor shall repair or replace any rejected work within seven days after receiving written notice.

NINE: Contractor shall not subcontract any part of the work without written consent of the Company.

TEN: Contractor shall have full control and direction over the mode and manner of performing the work.

ELEVEN: If, in the opinion of the Company's representative, the Contractor refuses or fails to supply a sufficient number of workmen, or the proper quantity or quality of material, or the necessary tools and equipment, or refuses or fails in any respect to carry on the work with promptness and diligence, the Company may give the Contractor written notice to remedy the default within 24 hours and, upon failure of the Contractor to remedy the default within such time, Company reserves the right to take over any or all labor, materials and appliances, to provide labor and material, and to complete or have completed any part or all of the work. The cost of completion by the Company shall be deducted from the unpaid balance, if any, due the Contractor under this Contract. If there is no unpaid balance, Contractor agrees to reimburse the Company for the cost of the completion.

TWELVE: Contractor expressly agrees not to discriminate against any employee or applicant for employment because of race, color, religion, sex or national origin.

IN WITNESS WHEREOF, Company and Contractor have executed this Contract in duplicate the day and year first above written.

_____

Company

_____

Contractor

## ATTACHMENT A

*Specifications for Monthly Newsletter*

Publication size:

11x17 inches, printed two sides, folded and stapled to make eight pages, 8½x11 inches.

Margins:

Top: 1 inch; bottom: ¾ inch; outside and inside: ¾ inch.

Column widths: 3 column—13 picas; 2 column—22 picas.

Headlines: 14-, 18-, 24- and 30-point Helvetica and Goudy.

Body copy:

10-point Times-Roman and 12-point Goudy Old Style with one point leading.

Paper stock: 60 lb. ivory, Scott offset vellum

Number of copies: 5,000

## ATTACHMENT B

*Schedule*

Step

(1)     1. Company will supply all typewritten copy to Contractor by noon on Monday of first week of month.

(3)     2. Company will supply all photographs, corrected galley proofs, page layouts, cutlines and headlines to Contractor by Friday of first week.

(5)     3. Company will supply corrected page proofs to Contractor by noon on Wednesday of second week of month.

(7)     4. Company will supply corrected proof sheets of newsletter to Contractor by 4 p.m. on Friday of second week.

(9)     5. Company will supply approved proof of newsletter to Contractor by 9 a.m. Tuesday of third week of month.

(2)     6. Contractor will supply typeset galley proofs to Company by 9 a.m. on Thursday of first week of month.

(4)      7. Contractor will supply four sets of page proofs and four sets of silverprints of photographs to Company by 9 a.m. on Tuesday of second week of month.

(6)      8. Contractor will supply corrected page proofs to Company by 4 p.m. Thursday of second week.

(8)      9. Contractor will supply proof of newsletter to Company by noon on Monday of third week of month.

10. Contractor will supply 5,000 copies of newsletter printed, trimmed, folded and stapled to Company by noon on Friday of third week.

11. Contractor will make all pickups and deliveries of material supplied by both Company and Contractor.

12. Contractor will provide paper and layout sheets.

13. Invoices will be submitted by Contractor to Company at the end of the month in which the work was performed.

14. Invoices will include:
>Base rate for 5,000 copies
>Number of halftones x $7.50 each.
>Typesetting, $30 x number of pages.
>Number of alteration hours x $15.
>Tax.

# Appendix 5
# Copy Editing Marks
# & Typesetting
# Specifications

# COPY EDITING AND PROOFREADING MARKS

| Mark | Meaning | Example |
|---|---|---|
| ∂ | delete; take out | Always mark ~~all~~ proofs |
| # | insert space | Always mark proofs properly. |
| ^ | insert letter(s) or word(s) | Always mak proofs properly. |
| ∽ (tr) | transpose letters or words | Always proofs mark properly. |
| ⊏ | close up; no space | Always m ark proofs properly. |
| ⊏ | align with left margin | ⊏ Always mark proofs properly. |
| ⊐ | align with right margin | ⊐ Always mark proofs properly. |
| ⊐⊏ | center | ⊐ Mark Proofs ⊏ |
| ¶ | start new paragraph | ¶ Always mark proofs properly. |
| no ¶ | do not start new paragraph | Always mark proofs. no ¶ Mark them properly. |
| ∼ | do not start new line | Always mark proofs properly. |
| stet | do not make correction; let stand as written | Always mark proofs ~~properly~~ stet |
| qv. | this is wrong; see copy | Always proper mark poof qv. |
| ? | this is questionable; check or query author | Never mark proofs properly. ? |
| ∧ | insert comma | Proofs ∧ if properly marked ∧ |
| ⊙ | insert period | Always mark proofs properly ⊙ |
| ∨ | insert apostrophe | The proofs in the proof marks. |
| ∨" | insert quotation marks | He said, ∨ Mark proofs properly. ∨ |
| =/ | insert hyphen | The writer =/∧ editor marks proofs |
| (—-) | insert dash | Always (—-)∧ not sometimes ∧(—-) mark |
| sp | spell out | Proofing is a (No. 1) priority. sp |
| // | align | Always mark proofs properly |

## Typesetting Specifications

| | |
|---|---|
| c/lc | Set in upper and lower case letters |
| (double underline) | SET ALL CAPS (upper case) |
| l.c. | set all lower case |
| (double underline) | SET IN SMALL CAPS |
| ital. | Set in italics |
| bf. | Set boldface |
| reg. rom. | Set regular roman |
| [ 12/14 ] | Set in 12-point type on 14 points leading; flush left and ragged right |
| [ ] | Set with both margins justified |
| ⅃ ⊏ | Center |
| 19 pi | Set 19 picas wide |
| 21 p/ | Set with longest line no more than 21 picas wide |
| ⊓ | Indent one em (the space of one M) |
| ⊓⊓ | Indent two ems |

## Copy Marking

### *Sample Marked Copy*

Here is an example of a story—a story is called *copy* when it is about to go into print—that has been edited and *specked*, i.e., marked with specifications for the typesetter. What you see is called *final copy*. Before the story got this far, you may be sure it went through extensive editing and revising stages that were not at all so orderly as this tidy sample.

When such copy comes back from the typesetter, it is accompanied by typeset galleys. You will read the galleys, comparing them with the copy to be sure that the galleys say what the copy says. You will need another person to proofread galleys with you—one will read the story while the other verifies that it is in the galleys as it was written, according to specifications.

*Title:*
[ 14/14 ]
*Bodini c/lc Bold*

*Body:*
[ 10/11 ]
*Bodini reg. roman c/lc*
19∅

This MD's Office/Makes House Calls

Doctor Trucks Trailer/To Homebound Patients

Each Tuesday morning, the residents of a Ft. Lauderdale
trailer park wait for their family doctor to make his regular
day-long stop there.

And he does--bringing along his office in a 40-foot
trailer.

Since he finished his family practice residency at the
University of Miami school of medicine in 1977, Academy member
James Andersen has not worked in a stationary medical office.
His mobility allows him to reach patients who are homebound or
who can't easily get to a doctor's office.

"I first got this idea back in 1970 as a medical student,"
Dr. Andersen said. "The school was just beginning to operate a mobile
coronary care clinic, and I thought, 'Why couldn't it be used
to care for any patients of limited mobility?'"

When he finished his residency, Dr. Andersen searched for
a site for his practice but found medical offices too expensive
"When you come out of residency, you're keyed up to do good
things, but you're also broke!" he said.

Recalling his idea, he bought and equipped a trailer.

Dr. Andersen parkes Tuesday through Friday at five trailer
parks and condominium areas ranging from 500 to 1,200 housing
units each. One trailer park is "really the size of a small
community," he said.

House Calls p. 2

A nurse/receptionist comes on board at 9:30 each morning after confirming patient appointments from her home.

Dr. Andersen pulls into the trailer park and plugs his office into the park's electrical system. He's then ready to see patients. While office hours are officially 9:30 a.m. to 5 p.m., he often stays into the evening, until the last patient is seen.

Although his office has all the diagnostic facilities of a standard medical office, Dr. Andersen has no telephone except at one park site. If he needs one, he uses a pay phone.

Patients wanting appointments leave messages on the doctor's home telephone answering machine. The ~~answering~~ machine gives his location each day so patients can find him in case of an emergency. Many patients just walk in, emergency or no emergency.

This unusual office arrangement is cost effective, "And it allows my practice to change with the times," Dr. Andersen said.

"In these hard times, a physician has to maintain as efective a practice as he can ~~consistent with good quality care~~. My trailer practice allows me to give high quality care with little overhead."

"Besides," Dr. Andersen added, "I have fun doing it!"

-30-

# INDEX

Abbreviations, defining, 55; when to use, 130

Accuracy, importance of in news reporting, 53; of overall impression made by story, 53; of word choice, 54

Achievements, as news source, 35

Acronyms, defining, 55

Active voice, use of in headlines, 75

Advocacy role of editor, 37

Apostrophe, use of, 121

Artists, hiring outside, 17

"Ascenders," various lengths of in typefaces, 90

Association newsletters, 9, 27 (see also Membership organizations)

Attribution, of news sources, 47, 30, 62; of emotional attitude, 53, 76

Audience, defining, 8, 27; multiple, 2, 33; keeping in mind, 7

Authority, agreed-upon for decisions, 21

Bidding policies, knowing and conforming to, 21

Births, deaths and weddings, as news in employee publication, 34

"Bleeding," ink through paper, 85

Body of news story, various forms of, 60

Boldface type, in headlines, 72, 143; as textbreaker, 104

Book reviews, 32

Boss, the overbearing, 22

Boxes, as page design amenities, 98, 103-5; in two-story stories, 61

Calendars, 35, 100

Capitalization rules, 124

Captions, photo, 97

Cartoons and comics, as features, 32

Circulation, widely scattered, 9; as factor in choice of copying method, 112, distribution method, 113

Civic promotions, as news features, 32

Circumlocutions, reducing to plain English, 54-55

"Clever" headlines, 74

"Clip art," using for graphic illustration, buying, 98

Colon, use of, 121

Column width, relation to type size & readability, 91

Comma, use of, 119; splice error, 137

Common errors, in sentence structure, 136; in spelling, 126-28; in usage, 52, 127

Community, readers as a, 27

Complex sentence, structure of, 134

Compound sentence, structure of, 135

Compound-complex sentence, structure of, 135

Community, readers as a, 27

Continuing series, as feature news, 30

Controversy, effect on credibility, 37, 62; as story element, 156

Copy editing, list of steps involved in, 66; marks, 169

Copy marking, marks, 169; sample marked copy, 170

Copyfitting, 100

Copyright laws, 65

Costs, of equipment, 14-16, 95; of typesetting vs. typewriting, 17; working with printer to hold down, 86, 112

"Counting" headlines, 79

Credibility, importance of, 62; loss of, 37

"Cropping" to improve photographs, 96

"Cute" headlines, 71

Cutlines (captions), to identify photos, 97

Dangling modifiers, 138

Dash, use of, 123

Dates, importance of using only current in stories, headlines, 76

"Deck" subhead, 78, 146

Delayed lead, 58

"Descenders," various lengths of in typefaces, 90

Dictionary, use of agreed-upon, 52; use with thesaurus, 56

Direct lead, 58

Display type, 89

Distribution of news publications, 113

Dummy, pattern for layout, 101-2

Editing, copy, elements of, 65

Editor, as one-person show, 13; as judge of news value, 41, 101; volunteer help for, 13; as advocate of special audience, 37; relation to boss(es), 21

Editorials, proper identification of, 32

Editorial tone, achieving the right, 7, 35

Elite type, measuring to fit space, 92

"Em," as measure of paragraph indent space, 94

Employee publications, 33; insider vs. outsider news in, 8, 33; special news columns in, 34; formula stories in, 151; as morale builder, 35; right tone for, 7, 35

Equipment, buying/finding in-house, 14, 16; expensive photo, 95

Exclamation point, use of, 121

"Fair comment," as defense to libel, 64

Faulty parallelism, 138

Feature stories, 33; as series, 30; elements/treatment of, 48

Files and filing systems, 44

First amendment, as qualified freedom, 63

Firsthand news gathering, 41-2

Form contract for printer, 161

Format, 85; flexible to carry different amounts of news in different months, 86; image projected by, 7, 85

Formula stories, samples of, democratic nature of, 151

Fragments, sentence, 136

Fused sentence, 136

Galleys, 20; proofing with original copy, 170

Gossip and criticism, facing squarely, 62

Gothic typefaces, 89

Grammar, basic structure of English, 133

Graphic illustrations and design amenities, 98

"Gray" text, uninviting, 19; breaking with boxes, screens, dramatic quotes, 104; with two-story story, 61

"Gushing," inadvisability of, in print, 36

Gutter, space between columns and pages, 91, 101

Halftones, photo; estimated cost of, 17, 113; represented by rubylith vinyl on pasteup, 111

Headlines, 71; active voice in, 75; written all caps, 78; counting to fit space, 79; "cute," 71; "clever," 74; "deck," 78; establishing basic styles for publication, 78; failed, 74; functions of, 72; "hammerhead," 78; how to write good, 75; "kicker," 78; "label," 74; model schedule, 143; placement and size as indicators of story importance, 72; use of puns in, 71; taken from story lead, 73; typeface sizes and styles for, 77, 88; samples of, 143-147; "standing," 23, 76

*Headlines and Deadlines*; as source for short headline words, 81

Help, professional, 16; bidding for services, 21, 112; volunteer, 13

Helvetica, example of sans serif typeface, 90

"Highlight" (. . .of month stories), as feature news series, 30

History, as feature news series, 31

Human interest stories, 49

Humor in news, as feature story material, 48

Hyphen, use of, 123

Incomplete constructions, 139

"Inhuman interest" stories, 49

"Inquiring photographer," as feature news series, 31

"Instant printers," 86, 112

Interviews, 41-7; by phone, 42; by mail, 43; in chance encounters, 42; homework for, 44; preparing questions for, 43; conducting successful, 45; use of tape recorder in, 45; consulting files before, 44; writing story from, 46; overcoming reluctance to conduct, 43

Italic type, 89

Italics, use of, 124

Items, short news, 60

"Jump lines," how to write, 103

"Jumped" stories, 103

Justified and unjustified margins, 92

"Kerning" type to squeeze headline, 79

"Kicker" subheads, 78, 145-6

"Label" headlines, 74, 76

Layout, copyfitting for, 100; dummy for, 101; purchasing inexpensive boards for, 110

Leads, direct, delayed, 58; rhetorical devices in, 58; six elements of, 57

"Leading," white space in relation to column width, 91; in copyfitting, 100, dummying, 101

Legal considerations, 63; in word choice, 56

Letter-style newsletters, timely and personal qualities of, ix, 19; common trouble with, ix; paper for, 86

Letters to the editor, starting column, 32

Libel, elements of, 63; defenses against, 64

Loyalty to organization, balanced w/credibility & integrity, 37

Mailing, lists, 114, computerizing, 114; rates, four classes of, 114; regulations, 115; address space, leaving during layout, 99, 101
Makeup, 94
Management announcements, tone of, 36
Manuscript preparation, rules for, 119
Margins, width for readability, 91; justified vs. unjustified (ragged right), 92
Masthead, what goes in the, 99
Meetings, as sources of news, 28, 152
Membership organizations, central role of newsletter in identifying and unifying distant members, 9; as "community," 27
Model headline styles (sample schedule), 143
Model stylebook, 119-140
Morale, role of employee newsletter in, 35
"Mug" shots, capturing character in, 96

Name and nameplate, 98
Naming the newsletter, 98
News, where to find in inside sources, 27; in outside sources, 29; what's appropriate in employee publications, 34; ignoring bad, 38; handling boring, 28; "pegs," 48
News gathering, firsthand, 41; by phone, 42; thorough, as aid to objectivity, 41
News stories, chronological, inverted pyramid, and structured forms of, 60; judging importance of, 41, 65, 101
News writing, 5 Ws and H of, 48, 57; accuracy in, 53; approaches in various stories, 47; attribution of sources in, 47; background information for, 41; elements of good, 53; humor in, 48; inadvisability of "gushing" in, 36; leads, 57; use of short words, phrases, sentences and paragraphs in, 54; use of sidebar in, 61, time element in newsletter, 49; building suspense in, 58; two-story story, 61
Newsletters, as private newspapers, 1; as sources of continuity and community, 5; instances in which crucially important, 5; need for, 5; deciding on general, specific and "interested" purposes of, 6; defining audience(s) of, 7, 27, 33; as total program of organization, 9; as advocate of organization, 37; image projected by, 7; readability of, 85; right "look" for, 85; in public relations context, 8
"Non-repro blue" ink, 110
Numbers, use of, 131

Objectivity, achieving, 41
Opinion columns, 32
Outside professional help, 16 (see also Professional services)

Page makeup, elements of, 94
Paper, color, weight, folds, 85; image conveyed by, 85; best for best price, 86
Paragraph length, appropriate for news writing, 54
Parentheses, use of, 122

Pasteup, professional vs. do-it-yourself, 109; basic tools for, 109; inexpensive boards for, 110

Period, use of, 119

Personnel announcements, as news stories, 28, 151

Photographs, 95; captions and cutlines for, 97; "scaling" to size, 97; cropping, 96; qualities of good, 95; file of, 45; rubylith vinyl in place of during pasteup, 111; of editor, 96

Photographers, 13, 16; "inquiring," 31; goals for, 95

Pica type, measuring to fit space, 92

Picas, measuring type in, 87, 92

Points, measuring type in, 87, 92

Present tense, use in headlines, 75

Press type, rub-on, 19, 72, 86

Printers, estimates from, 17; as paper supplier, 86; sample contract, 161; steps in working with, 164; choosing and using, 112

Privacy, right to, 64

Productivity, increasing, 36

Professional outside services, contracting for, 16, 21, 112; sample contract for, 161

Profiles, as news feature series, 31

Promotions of community drives, 32

Proofreading copy, 20, 170; marks, 169

Proportion wheel, scaling photos with, 97

Public relations, 8

Punctuation, rules of, 119-24

Puns, use of in headlines, 71

Puzzles, as feature items, 32

"Qualified privilege," as defense to libel, 64

Quotation marks, use of, 122

Quotes, direct and paraphrased in news stories, 46; emphasizing dramatic, 105; clarifying and enlivening boring or opaque meeting/report stories with, 28

"Ragged right" margins, 92

Readability, 85; of serif vs. sans serif type, 90; table, 92; of typewritten newsletter, 19; of typeset newsletter, 20

Readers, keeping in mind, 7; sparking interest of, 49; in a hurry, 54; hooking with suspense by a delayed lead, 58, structured story, 61; leading through "jumped" stories, 103; as community, 27; of multiple audience publications, 33; satisfaction in series, 30; wish to read about selves, 34

Reports, as news sources, 28; handling fat and boring in news writing, 154

Reporters, volunteer, finding and training, 13-16

Rewriting, goals of, 62

Right words, finding, verifying, 56

Rights, of news subjects, 64

Roman type, 88

Rumors, printing truth behind, 38

"Sans serif" typefaces, 90

"Scaling" photos, 97

Screens & screening, 105

Semicolon, use of, 120

Sentences, length appropriate for news writing, 54; types, 133-135; errors in structure of, 136

Series, news feature, 30-33
"Serif" typefaces, 90
Services, volunteer, 13;
   professional, 16, 21, 112,
   contract for, 161
Shield Laws, 65
Shifts in subjects, verbs, 139
"Sidebar," in a two-story story, 61
Simple sentence, structure of, 133
"Solo head," use on front page to
   draw attention to story on an
   inside page, 103
Specification marks, 170;
   "specking" for typesetter, 93;
   sample "specked" copy, 171
Specifications for newsletter, 112,
164
Speeches, as news source, 29, 153
Spelling, aids to, 126; frequently
   misspelled words, 128; words
   with common prefixes and
   suffixes, 129
"Standing" heads, for president's
   column, 23;  deadest of all, 76
"Straight" reporting, 47
"Stringer" reporter system, 14
Stylebook, importance of, 50;
   model, 119
Subheads, use of "kickers,"
   "hammerheads," and "decks"
   as, 78; samples of, 145-46

Tape recorder, use of in
   interviews, 45
"Text breakers," 104
Thesaurus, circumspect use of, 56
Time element, in infrequently
   issued publications, 49
Truth, as defense to libel, 64
Two-story story, use of, 61
Type, choice of faces for text, 86,
   91; serif and sans serif, 90; for
   headlines, 77, 88; styles: roman,
   italic, script, gothic and display,
88; "fonts" and "faces," 89; sizes
   in picas, points, inches, 87
Typesetters, estimates from, 17;
   steps in working with, 20;
   marking specifications for, 93;
   specification marks for, 170;
   sample "specked" copy for, 171
Typewriting vs. typesetting, 17
Typewritten newsletters, trouble
   with, ix; as handsome, timely
   and personal, 19

White space, left by leading in
   gutters and between columns,
   91, 101; in general page
   makeup, 101
Words, problem, 52; homonyms,
   127; commonly misspelled, 126,
   128; right choice of, 53, 56, 76
Writing (see News writing, Model
   stylebook)

"x-height," 90

This book has been set in Goudy Old Style, a remarkably handsome, versatile and readable typeface designed by Frederic W. Goudy in 1915. It is a personal style book face of grace, warmth and soft sparkle achieved by the slight curving of many strokes and the subtle styling of serifs. H. Marshall Wagoner III designed the book and Frances Baker Evans set the type and composed the pages.

*Marvin Arth* has degrees in law and journalism. He has reported, edited, and directed news for major newspapers and television stations in Cincinnati, Kansas City, San Francisco and New York. He has taught journalism at the University of Kansas and conducted newsletter workshops nationally.

*Helen Ashmore* has a master's degree in English and has taught writing at the universities of Kansas, Missouri, Hawaii and Northern Colorado. She has been an editor for Hallmark Cards and for *American Family Physician* magazine and has directed public relations programs for public and private organizations.